SQUIBBS' HISTORY OF BRIDGWATER

Squibbs' History of BRIDGWATER

Philip J. Squibbs

Revised and updated by

JOHN F. LAWRENCE M.A., M.Litt.

Phillimore

1982

Published by
PHILLIMORE & CO. LTD.
Shopwyke Hall, Chichester, Sussex

ISBN 0 85033 440 3

Printed and bound in Great Britain by
BILLINGS BOOK PLAN
Worcester

CONTENTS

LIST OF ILLUSTRATIONS

FOREWORD

This is not really a new book. It is an edited, re-compilation of the material that P. J. Squibbs published, in a remarkable 'do-it-yourself' hand-duplicated form in three volumes between 1957 and 1971. He had been too modest to offer his work to any of the national publishing houses and it was not until 1980 that his widow, Mrs. Dorothy Squibbs, decided to take this step in view of the increasing demand for some form of re-issue, 'properly printed'. At the suggestion of Mr. Keith Hardy, of the 'Rhyme and Reason' Bookshop, the specialist local history publishers, Messrs. Phillimore, were approached and they immediately recognised the importance of the Squibbs collection of photographs.

The collection is, of course, unique. The nucleus came from the archives of an old Bridgwater firm that closed down, mainly taken by professional photographers between 1860 and 1914. Philip Squibbs inherited them from his father and for the rest of his life became an avid collector of any other old photographs or postcards of Bridgwater that came his way, to add to the basic collection. Public interest grew and he decided that he wanted to be able to talk about the pictures and answer questions on them. Before he could do so he had to spend several years in research in our local libraries, the County Record Office, newspaper files and old directories. Though he had no formal historical training, he had one more important basic qualification. He knew and understood Bridgwater. His pride in its past is obvious in these pages.

After some years of talks and lectures he was persuaded to set his captions and text down in writing, to share the information with even more of his fellow townsmen. Quite remarkably, he acquired a duplicator and personally ran off all the pages of what became three substantial volumes. He did his own marketing, though that was not difficult as the books enjoyed great popularity despite their somewhat amateur appearance and typewriter typography. They have been used extensively as a valuable source for local history—for example by local schoolmasters and the press—but before reprinting them, in this new composite form, Phillimore thought it essential that someone with a working knowledge of Bridgwater history should undertake the task of checking facts and dates—not least to sort out errors resulting from changes since Mr. Squibbs wrote the original text.

Knowing that I had produced the official Town Guide and that I was deeply involved in research for my own, planned 'History of Bridgwater', the publishers approached me and I was delighted to be able to help to make Mr. Squibbs' invaluable work and pictures available again. I have not re-written P. J.'s work, but simply revised it, bringing together the essential text of all three original volumes. It was necessary to retrace his footsteps in checking the text, mainly in the libraries. We have only one library service, now, the County Library. All members of its staff are obliging and anxious to help anyone engaged in research. I am indebted to all of them, but to two in particular I offer a special note of thanks: Mr. Philip Stoyle, of Bridgwater, and Mr. David Bromwich at Taunton Local History Library.

It is certain that this fascinating collection of pictures will interest a far wider public than the local townspeople for whom it was originally intended, providing, as it does, a comprehensive record of the street scene and way of life of a rather unusual provincial town in the late 19th and early 20th centuries. In Bridgwater itself, a warm welcome for this book is assured, not least because it preserves a record of much that has disappeared. For example, two branches of trade important to Bridgwater at that time have both closed down—the docks and the brick and tile industry. Fortunately the docks are to be given a new existence and one old kiln is to remain standing. But many fine buildings have been demolished, many aspects of old Bridgwater have vanished, except in the pages of this book. Thus, Squibbs' History of Bridgwater makes an important contribution to the preservation of our heritage.

J. F. LAWRENCE
October 1982

BRIDGWATER VICTORIAN DAYS

BRIDGWATER WAS in those days a comparatively busy and flourishing manufacturing and agricultural town, with a port and railway station, situated on the River Parrett which was navigable for large ships, and ran in a winding course between Combwich and Huntspill towards the Bristol Channel at Burnham-on-Sea. It was one of the busiest maritime centres in the West of England, and tall-masted ships were a familiar sight. It was a period of prosperity in Bridgwater which had been a port for the past 500 years.

The town was pleasantly situated about nine miles from the sea, in level and well-wooded country; to the north-east are the Polden and Mendip Hills, and on the west the Quantock Hills. The River Parrett divides the town into two parts, connected by an iron bridge erected between 1795 and 1797 by the Coalbrookdale Company. It was subsequently replaced by the present bridge erected in 1883. The west part of the town was the larger. The streets were well paved, and lighted with gas; the houses were generally good (built of brick or stone), and some of the shops were very handsome. The other part of the town, called Eastover, improved much later when the railway station was there.

Bridgwater was in the hundred of North Petherton, Deanery and Union archdeaconry of Taunton, and the diocese of Bath and Wells. It was 151¼ miles distant from London, 44½ from Bath, 33 from Bristol, 42½ from Exeter, 95½ from Plymouth, and 25 miles from Yeovil.

Bridgwater is a very ancient town and its history can be traced back to Norman times. During the Civil War (1642-46) it was a royalist stronghold. The Castle was strongly fortified, having 40 large guns mounted on the walls. There was a deep moat about thirty feet wide which was filled with water at every tide. The Governor, Colonel Wyndham, had held his post for about three years when the Parliamentary Army launched an irresistible assault. On Wednesday, 23 July 1645, he was compelled to surrender. Vast quantities of arms and ammunition, 36 cannon, and over 1,000 prisoners were taken Another 2,000 men were allowed to march away without arms. A great quantity of jewels, plate and other articles of immense value were taken by the besiegers. The defences of the Castle were dismantled and even the residential part has since been entirely destroyed.

The inhabitants of Bridgwater supported the claims to the throne of the ill-fated Duke of Monmouth, a natural son of King Charles II; and he was proclaimed king by the Mayor and Corporation. The battle of Sedgemoor, the last battle fought on English soil near Westonzoyland in July 1685, resulted in the defeat of the rebel forces, headed by the Duke of Monmouth. The Duke was captured and executed; he made his survey of the King's forces gathered around the moors of Westonzoyland from the tower of St Mary's church.

Admiral Robert Blake (1599-1657) was born in Blake Street, Bridgwater, though it was not until 1900 that the statue to his memory was unveiled on the Cornhill, Bridgwater. The house of his birth was purchased by the town as a museum in 1924, having often been restored. Admiral Robert Blake's grandfather was thrice elected Mayor of the town.

The River Parrett was navigable to Bridgwater for vessels of up to 400 tons but was subject, like some other rivers in the Bristol Channel, to a rise of nearly six fathoms at spring tides. The flow of water is preceded by a head water commonly called the 'Bore', which rushes up the river with great force and often produces much inconvenience to ships. This head water is simply the first wave of the tide and is common to a very few rivers.

Bridgwater was a busy port with some important trading connections. The principal imports were coal, grain, timber, hides, and linseed, from the Mediterranean, France, Norway, Sweden, the United States, Canada, Newfoundland, Prussia and Russia. Coal was imported from Wales and other parts of the country and was brought up river to the Docks, to the Town Bridge, or to the West and East Quays. It was conveyed to different parts ot the country by river and canal. The river was navigable by barges along its branches to Glastonbury, Taunton, and Ilchester, and then into Devonshire.

The exports were cement, plaster of Paris, bricks, and tiles, as well as other goods manufactured in the town and district. One great source of employment was the manufacture of scouring brick, known as 'Bath Brick'; the trade was not carried on in any other place in England. The famous 'Bath Bricks' were made from a peculiar kind of slime which was deposited on the banks of the river near the Town Bridge. After every tide it was gathered, prepared, and made into the well-known bricks which were then familiar in almost every household as a valuable aid to cleanliness. Several milions of bricks were manufactured annually.

A large amount of shipping traffic was generated from Bridgwater, due primarily to the fact that the Severn Tunnel connecting England to South Wales by train was not then in existence. At the year end March 1861, for example, the number of foreign vessels carrying imported cargo totalled 31, while 11 were carrying export cargo. In the same year coasting vessels which carried imports totalled 3,473, while 1,212 carried exports. The total tonnage of vessels entering the river in 1861 was 158,919; and the duties on imports for the same year were £9,215. There were 195 vessels belonging to the port of Bridgwater, with a total tonnage of 14,191 tons.

The chief industries of the town in Victorian times were the manufacture of 'Bath Bricks', bricks and tiles, pottery and drain-pipes. There were also breweries, cement manufacturers, and iron foundries. The Bridgwater Ironworks of Messrs Hennett, Spink & Else were on a very extensive scale and gave employment to a large number of people, as did the Bristol and Exeter Railway Company situated near the railway station. Smaller industries included furniture and cabinet manufacturers, and wicker chair and basket manufacturers. The manufacture of plaster of Paris was started in Bridgwater in about 1855 by Messrs Barham Bros, who had erected steam mills for the purpose.

The town was a busy market centre for the surrounding agricultural district and large weekly markets were held on Wednesdays for cattle, pigs and horses at the Cattle Market, situated then at Penel Orlieu on the site of the present *Classic* cinema. The Cattle Market was moved to Bath Road in 1935 and since then the trade and business at the market has gradually declined. The weekly sheep market was held at West Street, and large numbers of sheep were driven to it from the surrounding districts, penned along each side of the street, and sold, usually by auction. The Sheep Market was also later moved to Bath Road. In the Market House Buildings on the Cornhill a market was held every Wednesday which was well attended, with stands for butter, poultry, meat, fish and vegetable produce. The Corn Market was also held there. There was also a small market on Saturdays for general produce such as vegetables, fruit, and meat. An Agricultural Show was held annually (Mr C. Babbage was the Secretary in 1861). This event is still held and is always a great success.

The town was then governed by a Mayor, six Aldermen and 18 Councillors, with a Recorder, Town Clerk, and Clerk of the Peace. The Borough Quarter Sessions were held in the Sessions Court of the Town Hall, and Borough Petty Sessions for the division of the county on the second and last Thursday of each month at the Town Hall at 11 o'clock.

The Borough Gaol and Police Station was in Fore Street and contained separate wards for both male and female prisoners. A police force of less than a dozen maintained law and order in the town. The police carried canes which were used to good effect on youngsters who caused any trouble. They also had to pay attention to street lighting and wastage of water. The Borough Gaol and Police Station was moved to the High Street in 1875 and to Northgate in 1911. The police arrangements were then under the control of the Corporation.

Population

1801	.. 3,634		1851	.. 10,883		1901	.. 15,168
1811	.. 4,910		1961	.. 12,120		1921	.. 15,962
1821	.. 6,155		1871	.. 12,636		1931	.. 17,139
1831	.. 7,807		1881	.. 12,704		1951	.. 22,221
1841	.. 10,430		1891	.. 12,419		1956	.. 23,700

St Mary's Church is a fine stone structure in the Perpendicular style with a tower and lofty spire containing a clock, eight bells and a set of chimes. The interior consists of the nave, two aisles, chancel and transept. All the pews are made of oak as is the pulpit. The church was restored between 1848 and 1857 and a new oak roof was put up which is much admired. One of the windows near the Corporation pews at the south end is of stained glass and was presented in 1852 by the late Thomas Ford, then Mayor of the town. In the chancel is a marble monument (a recumbent figure) to the Kingsmill family. The altarpiece is a picture of great beauty: it represents the 'Descent from the Cross', and was found on board a captured French privateer. It was presented by the late Hon A. Poulett, for many years M.P. for the borough. The painter is not known, but is supposed to be a French or Italian master. The spire is 200ft. high and was struck and damaged by lightning in 1894, and was repaired in 1897. At the same time two men were killed in Pounds Fields, Chilton, and a large brick kiln was damaged at Saltlands so that it had to be eventually demolished. The steeple was badly damaged in 1813, and a well-known local builder named Hutchings repaired it. He also built the Dome of the Market House, the National Provincial Bank on the Cornhill, College House in North Street, where he lived, and Hutchings Buildings in Mount Street. In 1887 the weathercock was re-gilded and the tower re-pointed; a local gentleman, Mr Brown, ascended the scaffolding to the spire and took photographs of the town.

There were three banks and one savings bank in the town in 1861; several good hotels with Assembly Rooms at the *Royal Clarence* hotel, Cornhill, and at the *Globe* hotel, Eastover. Two newspapers were published weekly in 1861, *The Bridgewater Standard* in St John Street, and *The Bridgwater Mercury and Western Counties Herald* in King Street.

The Gas Works situated in the Old Taunton Road was established in 1834 and was the property of shareholders.

The Bridgwater Infirmary, now the Bridgwater Hospital, situated in Salmon Parade was established in 1813 and accommodated 50 in-patients; it was supported by voluntary contributions.

Bridgwater was well supplied with reading rooms. There were three free reading rooms: one in Taunton Road established in 1856, one in St John Street established on 1 November 1860, which contained a library of standard works; and one in West Street which opened on 4 February 1861, and which also had a small library. They were all well supplied with daily and weekly London and provincial newspapers.

The Bridgwater School of Art in George Street was opened in January 1860. There was a literary and scientific institution in George Street containing a well-selected library of more than 1,500 volumes, besides the daily and weekly newspapers. There was also a museum there.

Fairs were held on the last Wednesday in January, March and June for horses and cattle; the last Wednesdays in September for horses and cattle; and the two following days for cattle and merchandise. Races were held annually in September.

The 28 June 1837, Coronation day of Queen Victoria, was a general holiday on which the Mayor and Corporation and others attended St Mary's Church and afterwards walked in procession through the streets of the town.

The Baptist Church in St Mary Street was rebuilt in 1837; it was founded in the 17th century. There is seating for 710 persons.

The Mariners' Congregational Church in St John Street was built originally for the use of seamen connected with the port. The last session of worship was held there on Sunday, 26 June 1960. The building is now in use as a garage.

West Street School was opened in July 1860. It was erected at a cost of £1,068 by grants, donations and subscriptions; a charge of 1d a week was made for children of ages varying from three to seven, and 1½d for the over-sevens. The school was closed in 1968 when the buildings were found to be in danger of slipping into the canal and has since been demolished.

The Congregational Church in Fore Street was built in 1862. This building was demolished in 1964, and Tesco supermarket (No 25 Fore Street) was built on the site. The members of the church moved to a new building, now known as the United Reformed Church, in West Street.

The Town Hall and Municipal Buildings in High Street opened on 6 July 1865. It was built on a site formerly occupied by the old Guildhall and Assize Court of Bridgwater brick and Wembdon Hill and Bath stone in the Italian style. The hall is capable of seating 500 persons–340 in the body of the hall, and 160 in the balcony. There was a Grand Jury room and a waiting-room for witnesses.

In 1871 a paper was started called *The Bridgwater Gazette,* printed in Tiverton. In 1885 the proprietorship changed hands and its title was altered to *The Bridgwater Independent*; it was printed in a small office in York Buildings. In 1886 it was sold to John Whitby & Sons and ran for many years as the recognised organ of the Liberal party. It ceased to exist after June 1933 when the proprietors of *The Bridgwater Mercury* purchased the copyright.

A highlight of Victorian days was the enquiries held in 1869 which resulted in the disenfranchisement of the borough of Bridgwater and due to which three M.P.s were unseated (see *Diary,* 1869).

Victorian Days

1. A view of the river, ships and the old Town Bridge in 1865. A large number of sailing ships can be seen berthed at the West and East Quays and a crane on the East Quay. The old bridge with high railings and gas lamps in the centre and at each side was demolished and the present one erected in 1883. Note the cobble-stones along Binford Place. The iron bridge in this view was erected in 1795-7 and was described as 'newly constructed of curious mechanism'. Above the porch of the *Royal Clarence Hotel* can be seen an iron plaque of the arms of the town which was brought from the old bridge. These were days of great prosperity in the town; the ships were a forest of rigging; the smell of pitch and pine gave an extra tang to the salty air; and the nearby taverns were filled with local mariners and seafaring men from various parts of the world. To the right was the famous old *Globe Hotel* which was destroyed by fire in 1875.

2. A view of the south side of High Street in 1865 looking towards the Cornhill with the barber's pole outside the barber's shop; beer barrels outside the *White Lion Inn*. The landlord was then D. Denman, the father of the late Mr Denman, farmer, of Haygrove Farm, Durleigh. The building on the right is Cockayne, Watchmaker and Jeweller.

3. (*left*) A view of St Mary Street looking towards St Mary's Church in 1865. Note the cobble-stones and the rough state of the road. The premises to the left belonged to Willis, the builder, now the Tudor Restaurant. Compare this tranquil picture of St Mary Street with the busy traffic and bustle of today. The street lamps were hung out over business premises and were first lit with gas on 22 May 1834; the Gas Works situated in Old Taunton Road were established in this year and were the property of shareholders.

4. (*below*) A view of the Cornhill, the Market House Buildings and Dome, and the *Royal Clarence Hotel* in 1865. The Market House and Dome was surrounded by iron railings leaving a pathway against the kerb; in 1883 the advisability of removing these railing was considered. After petitions for and against the idea were presented to the Town Council it was decided to retain the railings and they were afterwards gilded at the expense of the then Town Clerk (Mr James Cook). The railings were eventually removed by order of the Bridgwater Corporation on 20 September 1895. Admiral Robert Blake's statue had not then been erected—it was unveiled in 1900. The *Royal Clarence Hotel* was also known as *Longhurst's Hotel* (Mr Longhurst was then the Proprietor). It was the Conservative Party's headquarters and members stayed there during their visits to the town. The *Royal Clarence Hotel* was built in 1824 on the site of two small Inns, the *Angel* and the *Crown*.

5. A view of the Wilts and Dorset Bank (No. 14 Cornhill) in 1865. Standing in the doorway of the Bank is the Manager, Capt. John Ford, a well-known gentleman in those days and the Commanding Officer of the old Bridgwater Yeomanry. To the left was Best, Pawnbroker and Clothier (No. 15) and on the right was Rich, Watchmaker and Jeweller (No. 13). Nos. 14 and 15 (now fused into one shop) have been taken over by W. H. Smith & Sons Ltd.

6. A view of Penel Orlieu in 1865 with the old *Queen* licensed house, sometimes referred to as the 'Round House'. Looking ahead is the High Street with trees overhanging from St Mary's Churchyard. The white building to the left of the picture is the old police station, No. 50 High Street. It was evidently a unique occasion to be photographed in those days judging by the curiosity of the youngsters standing in the road.

7. A view of the River and old Town Bridge in 1865 with sailing vessels berthed at the West and East Quay and barges alongside Binford Place, the surface being entirely of cobble-stones. To the right is the cannon which was captured in the Russian War and presented to the town in 1857. In 1886 the gun was removed and placed on ground at the junction of the Bristol and Bath roads. On the right is the old *Globe Hotel* which was destroyed by fire in 1875. In 1875 the citizens of the town had a great thrill when they witnessed a 10 ft. 'Bore' sweep up the River; this is believed to be the highest head water ever recorded.

8. The paddle steam tug *Petrel* berthed alongside Carver's Shipyard on the East Quay in 1870. It was a cold winter as the floating blocks of ice show. The famous tug *Petrel* towed many sailing vessels up and down the river and was subsequently wrecked in a gale on Steart Island. The last vessel to be launched from Carver's Shipyard, East Quay, was the *Irene*.

9. A view of the River Parrett and Town Bridge in 1883 when there was an exceptionally high tide flooding the West and East Quays, Binford Place and Eastover. Water can be seen nearly to the top of the span of the bridge, and the barges could no doubt have floated in Binford Place. In 1883 a bank known as Baltmoor Wall in the Athelney district broke in three places and caused flooding up to a depth of eight feet in the district. The railway between Bridgwater and Durston was flooded causing great inconvenience and the loss to farmers and others was very considerable. The Somerset Drainage Commissioners afterwards raised a road which ran almost parallel to the wall in order to guard against a similar disaster.

10. A view of North Street which was flooded, probably after a thunderstorm, in about 1899. The old *Malt Shovel Inn* in the distance was pulled down and rebuilt in 1904. On Friday 8 March 1889 floods occurred in the town and district owing to the rapid thaw of deep snow. The Durleigh brook and other waterways overflowed their banks inundating Hamp Ward and damaging property, and also flooding several houses in Taunton Road. The inhabitants of Wembdon were also much inconvenienced.

11. A view of St Mary's church and the churchyard in 1865 with the black-faced clock. Note the darker portion of the steeple at the top which was badly damaged by lightning during a terrific thunderstorm in 1813. Note too the number of trees and shrubs in the churchyard. Restoration of the church commenced in 1850 at a cost of nearly £5,000; the seats were removed and replaced by new ones. Soon after this picture was taken, in 1867, a new clock was erected in the church tower and another bell, the eighth and largest, was hung. In 1871 a new organ was placed in the north chapel of the church at a cost of nearly £1,000.

12. A view of the old *Malt Shovel Inn* in North Street in 1865. This Inn was pulled down and rebuilt in 1904.

13. The junction of West Street and North Street looking towards Penel Orlieu in about 1890. The old Cattle Market gates in the middle distance are to the left of the man standing in the road. The building on the left of these gates was Gardiners' Dining Rooms. The building in the distance to the right of these gates was the *Mason's Arms*, an inn long since demolished. A noteworthy improvement took place in 1890 to the pig and cattle market which afforded accommodation for about 800 pigs and 300 calves. The work was carried out by Mr J. Palmer. The Cattle Market was opened at Penel Orlieu in 1875.

14. The north side of High Street in about 1890. The *Old Oak Inn* is on the right and the *Bull and Butcher Inn* on the left. R. J. Beer's Cycle Stores and a Hairdresser's establishment is next door. These old buildings had replaced the Shambles. They were all rebuilt *c.* 1905 but by 1980 both inns were closed and the buildings are now threatened with demolition under a development scheme.

15. A view of Friarn Street in 1865. Friarn Street was named after the Grey Friars who settled in Bridgwater in the 13th century. The wall and tree on the right have gone, together with the house that stood behind them. The site is now occupied by the G.P.O. Sorting Office.

16. (*opposite above*) The north side of Eastover near the Town bridge in 1865. The corner shop, No. 1 Eastover (now Wigfall's), belonged to Smith, Grocer and Provision merchant. To the right are Mole, the Chemist and J. Waddon & Sons an Ironmongers and Rope shop. All these premises changed hands and were rebuilt many years ago.

17. (*opposite below*) Thompson Bros., the Ironmongers shop on the south side of the Cornhill in 1865. The firm moved away from No. 4 Cornhill which is now a supermarket. It is reputed to be the oldest business in Bridgwater. It was in 1894 that the promoters of the half holiday movement in Bridgwater held a meeting under the presidency of the Mayor and as a result the tradesmen generally agreed to close their establishments every Thursday afternoon throughout the year. This was described as 'an undertaking which was honourably fulfilled and without apparently creating the slightest public inconvenience, whilst employers and assistants alike were appreciative of the opportunity for rest and recreation thus afforded'.

SHIPPING SUPPLIED
MOLE
CHEMIST
MOLE

18. Taunton Road looking towards the town from the Canal bridge in 1865. There are no houses on the right and those on the left are in course of construction.

19. A view of Castle Street in about 1865 from the river end with two trees in the roadway which have since been removed. The houses on the north side of this street were built by the Duke of Chandos, hence Chandos Street. Castle Street has been described as 'one of the most typically Georgian streets outside Bath'. The Mary Stanley County Training Home for nurses and the Bridgwater District Nursing Association was opened in 1902 in Castle Street as a memorial to Queen Victoria; one of the original objects of the Home was to supply a nursing service to poor patients in their homes without charge.

20. The old Bridgwater Workhouse on the Taunton Road situated opposite Holy Trinity church in 1865. The lettering on the wall reads 'Westropp for ever'. Mr Westropp was one of Bridgwater's M.P.s though he was eventually unseated at the bribery commission in 1869.

21. The entrance gates of the old Bristol and Exeter Railway Company's Carriage Sheds in 1865. These premises absorbed a large number of workpeople to build and repair railway carriages and trucks. Note the broad gauge railway lines behind the gates and the foreman with his top hat. When the railway was handed over to the Great Western Railway Company these premises were closed and the town received a great blow from which it did not recover for some years.

22. A picture of the Docks in 1868. On 25 March 1841 when the Docks were opened, a public holiday was celebrated in Bridgwater. At half past six in the morning the tide came up and entered the outer Dock rapidly amid the cheers of spectators. The tug *Endeavour* steamed down the river with a party of ladies and gentlemen and a band to meet the first ship to enter the Dock, which was the *Henry* of Bridgwater. The vessel sailed into the Dock amid the cheers of several thousand spectators, the roaring of cannon, the ringing of bells and the strains of the national anthem. The event was celebrated by a dinner at the *George Hotel* and at the *Royal Clarence Hotel*. The docks were afterwards purchased by the Great Western Railway Company who in 1870 connected them with their line by a telescopic bridge over the river. In 1869 the Bridgwater Oil and Cake Mills at the Docks were started, at first only about fifteen workmen were employed though eventually up to seventy men worked there. The Mills are now closed.

23. A picture of Northgate Brewery in 1865. The first annual meeting of Starkey, Knight & Co. Ltd., Brewers, of North Petherton and Bridgwater was held in October 1888 when the whole of the £100,000 capital was subscribed and substantial dividends were paid to the shareholders. The site of the Brewery was acquired by Sedgemoor District Council and since 1974 the brewery buildings have been demolished and local government offices erected.

24. A view of High Street in 1865 looking towards the *Royal Clarence Hotel*, Messrs Thompson & Rowe, Wholesale Grocers, now the Avenue and the premises of Boulting, Glass and China Warehouse, now a take-away food shop, No. 10 High Street.

25. East Quay in 1865 with goods spread along the Quay after being unloaded from ships. The Post Office was then in East Quay next to a Temperance Hotel. By the Post Office was Harwood's Timber and Slate Mills, now Messrs. Bradford's. East Quay was then a very busy thoroughfare with the loading and unloading of ships. Further along the Quay was the shipbuilding yard of Messrs. Carver, now closed.

26. The old Toll Gate and Toll House on the Durleigh Road in 1865. Each toll gate in the town had a Collector and tolls were collected for the entrance and exit of horse drawn vehicles. This building was situated at the top of Durleigh Hill and the nearest house looking towards the town then was the *Horse and Jockey Inn.*

27. A picture of Bridgwater station on the Bristol & Exeter Railway Line in 1865 with the horse omnibus outside waiting for passengers to be taken to the town centre. The *Railway Hotel* was built in 1841 and was popular with travellers. The Liberal candidates at elections usually made it their temporary residence. In 1842 the Bristol & Exeter Railway Company constructed wharves and sidings at Dunball, which facilitated the discharge of heavy imports of coal from vessels into trucks for distribution by rail throughout the West country.

28. The old toll gates at the junction of the Bristol and Bath Roads, off Monmouth Street, in 1865. The toll collector is about to collect the toll and a lad is opening the gates. There were then very few houses in the Bristol and Bath Roads; most of the houses in Bristol Road were built in 1887.

29. The premises of Stokes, Stationer, Bookseller and Publisher of a local newspaper called *The Bridgwater Standard*, at the corner of Fore Street and Court St reet in 1865. This is now part of Timothy White's, No. 14 Fore Street. Later these were the premises of *The Bridgwater Mercury*. It was the scene of a disastrous fire in 1883, as a result of which the then editor's wife and their three children lost their lives. It happened on Sunday 29 July 1883; the premises of *The Bridgwater Mercury* were found to be on fire, the flames spread rapidly to the lower portion of the house occupied by Mr Dunsford, the editor, and before assistance could arrive three of the children were burnt to death. Mrs Dunsford tried to save her life by throwing herself from a window on to a bed, but she fell on the pavement and sustained injuries from which she died. Mr Dunsford had a narrow escape but he was saved by the brave assistance of two Post Office officials, named Friend and Coll, who rescued him from a window. For their conspicuous bravery these two men were afterwards presented with marble timepieces by public subscription.

30. The old Toll Gate and Toll House on the Taunton Road in 1865. The old Toll House still stands opposite the *Hope Inn*. There were then very few houses along the Taunton Road.

31. The old Toll Gate and Toll House on the Wembdon Road in 1865. The Toll House still stands and in 1890 it was the Wembdon Police House. It is near the borough boundary.

32. Eastover, looking towards the Town Bridge in 1865. The old *Queen's Head Inn* is on the left and Phelps's *Commercial Hotel and Posting House* is on the right.

33. The old *Lamb* inn, High Street 1865, one of the oldest hostelries in the town; now the *Duke of Monmouth*.

34. The old Post Office at East Quay in 1865. The Post Office was later transferred to High Street and subsequently to the Cornhill in 1909. The tall postman was named Dell who used to do the Wembdon round; the postman in the centre was Lockyer; the Postmaster was W. T. Mitchell.

35. Eastover from the Town Bridge in 1865. On the left is Smith, York House, Grocer and Provision Merchant, now Wigfall's (No. 1 Eastover) and on the right is the famous old *Globe Hotel* which was destroyed by fire in 1875. This is now the Y.M.C.A. building.

36. The unveiling of the statue to Admiral Robert Blake which took place on Thursday 4 October 1900. It was unveiled by the Rt. Hon. Lord Brassey K.C.B. The Mayor, Alderman T. Good, accepted the statue on behalf of the burgesses of the town. A procession was formed at St John's Hall, Monmouth Street, which proceeded via Eastover, Binford Place and Dampiet Street to Blake Street where a tablet was unveiled by Lord Brassey at Admiral Blake's birthplace. At 2 p.m. a great banquet was held at the Town Hall and a luncheon was served to about two hundred and fifty guests and principal subscribers, at which the chair was taken by the Mayor. It was in August 1898 that a public meeting affirmed the desirability of erecting a statue in Bridgwater, his birthplace, to Admiral Blake and an influential committee was appointed with the Mayor (Alderman Foster) as President. The committee was very energetic and a sum of more than £800 was promised. In 1888 a movement was inaugurated in London for the purpose of providing a Memorial to the great Admiral Blake, and later St Margaret's Westminster was enriched by a stained glass window.

37. Fore Street from the Town Bridge in 1865 with the old *Castle Inn* to the left, a famous hostelry of seafaring men, now Nationwide Building Society (No. 2 Binford Place). On the right is the large premises of Akerman's Music and Piano Warehouse, now Halford's (No. 8 Fore Street). To the left opposite Akerman's is the old Bridgwater Gaol.

38. The old Sheep Market in West Street. In 1857 an Act of Parliament was obtained to rearrange the days of the Market and Fair; market day was to be on Wednesdays instead of Thursdays and St Matthew's Fair was to be on the last Wednesday in September. The Bridgwater Farmers' Association had discussed the advisability of altering the market day to better suit the convenience of agriculturalists as well as merchants and townsmen. The Cattle and Sheep Markets were both moved to Bath Road in 1935 and from thence on the trade and business at the Bridgwater Market gradually declined.

39. (*left*) View of a large sailing vessel at the East Quay in 1865. The gentleman with the top hat is the late Mr Robert Squibbs, Auctioneer and Estate Agent and author of *Auctioneers and their Duties*.

40. (*below*) North Street looking from the junction to West Street in 1865 where the old West Gate previously stood.

41. A view of Blake Street in 1865 with Blake House, the birthplace of the famous Admiral Robert Blake on the right. The house is now the Bridgwater Museum and was purchased by the town as such in 1924. It has been restored on many occasions.

42. The staff standing outside the Booking Office of Bridgwater station, on the Bristol & Exeter railway line, in 1859. The staff comprised the railway signalman (in the centre with top hat), three porters, and a boy. The year 1841 was important in the history of Bridgwater as the town was then connected with Bristol by the Bristol & Exeter railway. The line was opened on Whit Tuesday, 1 June, with great rejoicings. At 9 a.m. a vast crowd at the Bristol terminus saw the engine *Fireball* leave for Bridgwater and it arrived at the station amid loud and enthusiastic cheers as practically the whole town had turned out to welcome the train. The band of the West Somerset Yeomanry hailed the approach of the train with appropriate music. The journey took one and three quarter hours with no stops. Outside Bridgwater Station the *Railway Hotel* was being built. The occasion was celebrated by a sumptuous repast at the *Railway Hotel*. About a year later the railway was extended to Taunton and was later acquired by the Great Western Railway with subsequent extensions to many parts.

43. Holy Trinity Church, Taunton Road in 1865, before the Vicarage was built. The church was built in 1839. The church was demolished in 1958 when Broadway was created in order to bring the A39 straight to North Street.

44. A view taken in 1865 of St John the Baptist church in Blake Place, Eastover. It was erected by the Rev. John Moore Capes M.A. of Shipton-Moyne and consecrated on 17 August 1846. It is a handsome structure of bath stone and is in the early English style of architecture. The cost of erecting the church was between £5,000 and £6,000. The view illustrates the church before the pinnacles were added to the top of the tower in about 1890; the cost of which was met by the generosity of the Rev. Ruddock, a well-known clergyman of those days. Standing in the grounds is the Rev. Collins with his wife and daughter. All Saint's church, Westonzoyland Road, connected with St John the Baptist church, was built in 1882.

45. A busy sunny day in Fore Street looking towards Eastover in 1865 showing horse-drawn traffic and a near hold-up with parking each side. In 1878 work commenced on the reservoir on Wembdon Hill and water pipes were laid in Fore Street and, because the thoroughfare was so narrow the traffic had to be diverted through the side streets which caused some inconvenience. It was on 2 December 1879 that the Water Works at Ashford were opened at a total cost of £40,000. Fore Street today is still the same width. The picture was probably taken on a market day; the sun blinds are out and some of the men are in their shirt-sleeves.

46. Another view of the old Town Bridge and River Parrett in about 1865. In 1845 an Act was passed to improve the navigation of the river and the bay, to maintain the bridge and extend the quays, and regular dues and tolls were fixed for vessels entering the port. As the ships discharged one cargo, so another cargo of exports from the expanding local industries waited to be taken aboard. In 1886 the Bridgwater shipping trade suffered a big blow due to the opening of the Severn Tunnel; it caused a great change in the life of the port because coal traffic from South Wales no longer needed to be shipped to England.

47. The original Bridgwater Infirmary in Salmon Parade (previously Salmon Lane) in about 1865. The Infirmary then accommodated 50 in-patients. To the left is the old *Salmon Inn*, proprietor J. Kiddle, the site of which is now used by the Hospital. To the extreme left is the *Parrett Inn.* The origin of Bridgwater Hospital dates back to 1813 when a public meeting decided that a medical institution be established 'for the relief of the labouring poor requiring medical and surgical assistance'. In 1820 it was agreed to purchase a 'spacious house and garden' in Salmon Lane for £700. The Infirmary was then supported by voluntary contributions. Alterations and additions were made to the Infirmary in 1862 and soon afterwards an adjoining house was purchased for £205. Additions were again made in 1876 and 1895.

48. The ancient house 'Marycourt' in St Mary Street in 1865, where Judge Jefferies is said to have lodged during the trials at the 'Bloody Assize'. To the left were premises which were opened in 1871 by the Young Men's Association. The Association was started with a view to providing the means for the social recreation and enjoyment of the young men of the town. The premises contained a billiard room with two good tables, a spacious reading room etc. It was moved to Castle Street under the title of 'The Castle Club' and subsequently closed. To the right was the residence of John Bowen, the editor of a local newspaper called *The Bridgwater Alfred* and a man of strong political opinions.

49. (*above*) The beautiful residence above was Mrs Alexander's School for Girls in Friarn Street in about 1870. It is evidently 'Games' time, the pupils have hoops, croquet mallets and the bow and arrow board. Note the crinolines and bonnets. The G.P.O. Sorting Office now occupies this site.

49a. (*right*) Detail from above.

50. (*left*) A view of St Mary's church steeple from Friarn Street in 1878 when some alterations and repairs were done to the church showing scaffolding and steeple-jacks at the top. The cost of the alterations was about £2,000. Improved lighting was installed in the church with brass standards. The blue lias paving was removed and replaced with tiles; a heating apparatus was installed; the pillars and arches were scraped and cleaned which necessitated the closure of the church for six months. The spire is 200 ft. high and is a notable landmark which can easily be seen for miles in every direction.

51. (*below*) The *Globe Hotel* , Eastover, after the disastrous fire on 31 May 1875. It was an old coaching house and popular hostelry and was the headquarters of the Liberal party. The ruins were left in a derelict state for seven or eight years until they were cleared to make room for the Sir George Williams Memorial Hall (The Y.M.C.A. buildings) in 1905. After the fire these premises were let to auctioneers and others as storehouses. The site was sold on 30 September 1882 for £1,000 by public auction.

52. (*above left*) Shop premises in about 1865 at the corner of Coffee House Lane, (in 1890 Queen Street and now Court Street) and Fore Street, looking from King Street. The premises were later the offices of *The Bridgwater Mercury* which was first established on 18 June 1855; the first editor was George Thomas Donisthorpe, and it was printed and published in King Street. On 25 July 1883 a disastrous fire destroyed the above premises and unfortunately the earlier files of the newspaper were all destroyed in the blaze. *The Bridgwater Mercury* has never at any period in its existence lost its foremost position as the leading local newspaper. It is well supported by advertisers and its circulation has extended far beyond the town.

53. (*above right*) The old Bridgwater Gaol, Fore Street in 1865. The old gaol was closed and moved to the Police Station in High Street in 1875, and thence to Northgate in 1911 when the stone was laid by the Mayor, Mr H. W. Pollard on 3 August.

. The River Parrett frozen
er in the winter of 1895. The
ture shows townsfolk roasting
ox on the ice almost under
Town Bridge, with a large
mber of spectators watching
proceedings from the bridge.
advertisement in *The Bridg-
ter Mercury* dated 20 February
95 reads, 'A great novelty.
otographs of the frozen river
rrett with the bonfire and
wd on the ice, Unmounted
; Mounted 1/6d; size 8″ x 6″.
good Agent wanted to push
sale of them. A. Squibbs,
otographer, 38 Fore St,
dgwater.'

55. (*left*) The old Police Station, No. 50 High Street, in 1880. This building was later taken over by Mr W. H. Boys, Auctioneer and Estate Agent, and was pulled down in 1930. The Police force in 1860 comprised less than a dozen men to maintain law and order in the town.

56. (*below*) A picture of the Cornhill tastefully decorated in May 1883 on the occasion of the Bath and West of England Society annual show in Bridgwater. The affair was most successful throughout the week and the attendance of visitors far exceeded expectations. The town was beautifully decorated and a large amount of enterprise and enthusiasm was displayed by the townspeople. In 1851 the Bridgwater Agricultural Association held its first show at Blacklands in the town.

57. A view of the High Street and the *Royal Clarence Hotel* also known as *Longhurst's Hotel* in 1865. Mr Longhurst was the proprietor who left in 1866 and was followed by Mr Leaker who moved from the *Golden Ball Hotel* in High Street. Next to the *Royal Clarence*, at No. 10 High Street there was a china and glass warehouse of which Mr Boulting was the proprietor. Further along were Thompson & Rowe, wholesale grocers, now The Avenue.

58. St Mary Street looking towards the Market House buildings in 1865. Parsons, the Bakers', was alongside the back entrance to Thompson's Ironmongers' shop.

59. Dampiet Street in 1865. The large chestnut tree is in the grounds of Dampiet House, then the residence of George Payne, solicitor. The Unitarian church is on the right.

60. The east side of the Cornhill in 1865. The building with railings at the front was a chemist's shop, now the Leeds Building Society, No. 23 Cornhill. In 1840 there was a fire when two houses opposite the Market House on the Cornhill were burnt to the ground; fortunately there was no loss of life.

61. The old *Queens Head Inn*, Eastover, 1865.

62. The old *Three Tuns Inn*, Penel Orlieu, 1865. It was later demolished and became the site of part of the old Cattle Market and later the Classic Cinema and car park. To the right was the old *Mason's Arms Inn* which was also demolished to build part of the present Classic car park.

63. (*top*) A view of the River Parrett at Crowpill in 1865, the tugboat *Petrel* towing a sailing vessel.

64. (*centre*) A view of the Cornhill looking north-east in 1865. The premises in the centre was a chemist's shop, Good & Wilton, formerly Rueben C. Payne and before that William Snook. To the right are the premises of Shrimpton & Halson, Ironmongers. There is no traffic in sight.

65. (*bottom*) The beautiful residence and grounds of Dampiet House, Dampiet Street in 1865, then occupied by Mr George Payne, solicitor. The house is now turned into flats and the garden is a shopper's car park.

66. The residence and grounds of Halesleigh, Wembdon, 1865. Built in 1830 as the house of Thomas Clark, celebrated botanist (1793-1864), it belonged later to Mr G. B. Metford, then to Col. Trevor and eventually to Mr H. J. Squibbs. No longer in Wembdon, it is now the *Quantock Gateway Hotel.*

67. South side of the Cornhill, *c.*1865. The building on the extreme left is now No. 12 Cornhill (Hodge's); No. 11 (John Collier) is marked with a cross; No. 10 is Barclay's Bank (scheduled to move to No. 16 High Street), and on the extreme right, No. 9 is Lipton's. The cross denotes that George Williams, founder of the Y.M.C.A. movement, worked here as an apprentice to W.H. Holmes, a draper. In 1870 a disastrous fire destroyed the two buildings in the centre. When they were rebuilt, they were raised to four storeys and designed to resemble No. 9, which had been built *c.*1830-40. It was in January 1859 that George Williams established the Y.M.C.A. on the Cornhill. *(Photo: Courtesy of Miss D. Smith.)*

68. A view of the Cornhill and Market House buildings in 1865. There were only horse-drawn vehicles in those days, cobble-stones at the kerbside and very few street lamps. It was in 1870, on the night of 7 February that a destructive fire began on the south side of the Cornhill. The alarm was raised on the premises of Messrs Moore, Blacker & Moore, drapers, but the fire spread so rapidly that the adjoining shop and house of Mr John Whitby was soon in flames as well. The inmates were just retiring to rest but fortunately no lives were lost. Mr Whitby and an assistant named Miss Debac had a very narrow escape and were rescued from the roof of Messrs Moore's premises by means of ladders, by Mr Henry Wills, a chimney sweep and another man unknown. Both houses were burnt to the ground, and quantities of valuable goods were lost, the total damage was between £10,000 and £12,000; quite a substantial sum in those days.

69. The laying of the foundation stone of the new Post Office on the Cornhill in 1897. It was in July that the Post Office authorities entered into occupation of their new premises on the Cornhill, although the old premises in High Street which were rented from the Bridgwater Corporation continued to be occupied and used as a sorting office for the next four or five years until the expiration of the existing lease. The Post Office was originally on the East Quay before it moved to High Street and thence to the Cornhill.

70. A view of the Docks in 1898. In 1886 an important improvement took place when the dock gates were repaired and the docks and canal were cleaned. As many as 500 men were employed to do this and the quantity of mud removed was estimated at something like 130,000 tons. Unfortunately the docks and canal remained closed for six weeks in the busiest season of the year and there was reason to fear that much of the traffic which was sent through the Severn Tunnel in the meantime was permanently diverted.

71. A picture of a squibbing display at Guy Fawkes Carnival. Enthusiasm for the Carnival had lapsed before 1893 but in this year it was revived with much spirit and its success was almost unprecedented, though marred, unhappily, by a couple of serious accidents. In 1897 something in the nature of a mild sensation was caused in the town by the refusal on the part of the borough magistrates to grant the customary application for an extension of licensing hours on the night of 5 November, the occasion of the Guy Fawkes Carnival. A resolution was passed by the Bridgwater Corporation expressing regret at the decision and as a result the licensed houses were kept open as usual without any interference by the police authorities. (*Photo: Courtesy of Mr S. W. Palfrey.*)

72. The north side of Fore Street in 1865 showing Shrimpton & Halson, Ironmongers , now the premises of Marks & Spencer. To the right were the premises of Symons, tailor, outfitter, silk mercer and hosier, now an extension of Marks & Spencer.

73. A view of the River and the old Town Bridge in 1865. This bridge was erected in 1795-97 by the Coalbrookdale Company and was one of the earliest iron bridges in England. After almost a century of use it was found inconvenient and steep at the approaches and in 1883 it was removed to make way for the present structure.

74. A view from Durleigh Road looking towards the town in 1865. There were then few houses in Durleigh Road, the nearest facing the town being the *Horse and Jockey Inn.*

75. Premises on the Cornhill, Messrs. Nicholls & Co. in 1865, now Lipton's (No. 9 Cornhill). Next door, to the left, are the premises of Messrs. Whitby's, the scene of a destructive fire in 1870.

76. (*right*) The north side of Castle Street looking towards the river in 1865. It has been described as one of the most beautiful streets in the town. The houses, erected by the Duke of Chandos, are early Georgian. There were trees at the river end, since removed.

77. (*centre*) Harwood's Slate and Timber Wharf on the East Quay in 1865, now Messrs. Bradford's.

78. (*bottom*) Taunton Road looking towards the canal bridge from the town in 1865.

79. A view of North Street in 1865 with the old *Malt Shovel Inn* in the distance. The old man n the top hat standing behind the railings of the house on the right was Mr Hutchings, the uilder. He built College House, the Dome of the Market House, the National Provincial Bank n the Cornhill and Hutchings Buildings in Mount Street. College House has since been demol-shed. The site is now occupied by A. & S. White with a filling station and car showrooms.

80. The Cornhill and the *Royal Clarence Hotel* in 1865. A two-horse omnibus is leaving the *Royal Clarence* for the station. Railings then surrounded the Market House buildings and Admiral Robert Blake's statue had not then been erected. The *Royal Clarence Hotel* was originally named the *Royal Hotel* but the Duke of Clarence (afterwards William IV) changed horses at the *Royal*, and permission was asked of the illustrious stranger to name it the *Royal Clarence*, which was readily granted.

81. Shop premises in Fore Street in 1865; Symons, tailor, outfitter, silk mercer and hosier, now part of Marks & Spencer's premises.

82. Wembdon Road from Northfield in 1865. There are no houses on the left and cemetery railings on the right. In the distance is Halesleigh Tower, now the *Quantock Gateway Hotel.*

83. (*above*) The shop of Mr Archibald Graham, stationer and bookseller, in 1865, on the corner of Fore Street and George Street. These premises were formerly occupied by Poole, later by Belcher and then by W. H. Smith & Sons Ltd. W. H. Smith's have now moved into Nos 14 and 15 Cornhill. Standing in the doorway are Mr John Ford, Mr Graham and Dr. Parsons.

84. (*right*) Shop premises at the corner of Eastover and East Quay near the Town Bridge in 1865, occupied by Smith, grocer and provision merchant, now Wigfall's, No. 1 Eastover. The premises were then called York House and quite a substantial business was done supplying ships' stores.

85. A view of the Docks in about 1898. In 1893 the Port and Navigation Committee of the Town Council devoted much time and anxious consideration to the gradual diminution of the shipping trade of the port, as the number of vessels entering Bridgwater had fallen off from 3,300 in 1890 to 2,531 in 1892, a decrease of 769 in two years, making a decreased tonnage of 30,000 tons. The explanation was that most of the coal traffic from South Wales had been diverted through the Severn Tunnel.

86. Binford House, Binford Place in 1895, the residence of R. C. Else, Esq., Mayor in 1897. Binford House is now the site of the Bridgwater Public Library. This residence and Blake Gardens were purchased from Mr Else in 1898 by the Bridgwater Corporation. The gardens consist of about two and a half acres of ground on the west bank of the river in the centre of the town. They are beautifully laid out with lawns and flower gardens and contain some fine chestnut trees. The Public Library, erected through the generosity of Andrew Carnegie, was opened in 1906. The Roman Catholic church in Binford Place, fronting the river and dedicated to St Joseph, was built in 1882.

87. (*above*) A view of the beautiful residence, The Priory, St Mary Street in 1865. These buildings are now used as offices by the Sedgemoor District Council.

88. (*right*) The old *White Horse Inn*, Penel Orlieu, in 1865, once an old coaching inn. Now the site is occupied by the premises of the Bridgwater Co-operative Society.

89. A tea party on the frozen River Parrett in 1895, near Bridgwater.

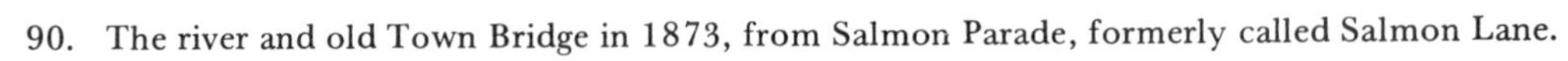

90. The river and old Town Bridge in 1873, from Salmon Parade, formerly called Salmon Lane.

91. A view of the river and Town Bridge from the West Quay in 1896, showing quite a number of ships including the old tug *Petrel* to the left.

92. A picture of the celebration of the Golden Jubilee of Queen Victoria on the Cornhill on 20 June 1887. (*Photo: Courtesy of Mr S. W. Palfrey.*)

93. The premises of Hook, grocer and provision dealer at No. 14 Fore Street, in 1865. This is now Timothy White's.

94. The old *Castle Inn* at the corner of Fore Street and Binford Place in about 1878. This Inn was a famous hostelry of seafaring men in Victorian days. It is now the Nationwide Building Society, No. 2 Binford Place. (*Photo: Courtesy of Mr S. W. Palfrey*.)

A BRIDGWATER DIARY

1800 THE POPULATION of the town was about 3,500. There were no houses west beyond the *Malt Shovel* inn and none beyond the old *Queen's Head* inn in Estover. The now busy St John Street was a field where local cricketers held their matches. The Post Office, a little general shop, stood on the Cornhill. Letters and parcels came from London every evening by stage coach between five and six o'clock, together with the only London newspaper that reached the town—and that a day late. The Postmaster was in the habit of copying out items of interesting news and displaying them outside, the result being that crowds of people were to be found there every evening, eager for news of the big world beyond. The few letters for the town were afterwards delivered by an old woman.

The old stone bridge over the river had been demolished in 1795-97 and a new iron bridge erected and officially opened in 1797 by the Mayor, Mr Robert Codrington, who resided at Ivy House, Friarn Street. The Borough coat-of-arms was conspicuous on the bridge, as was the inscription 'R. C. Mayor 1795'.

Only one of the old town gates was still standing—the South gate. It stood across St Mary Street at the point where the Old Taunton Road veers to the south-east, leaving the present Taunton Road. The North gate had stood at the end of Angel Crescent. The East Gate had been at the end of Eastover, some yards before the road turns north into Monmouth Street. The West gate used to stand at the entrance to Penel Orlieu at its junction with North Street.

The oldest streets were High Street, Fore Street, Friarn Street, Dampiet Street, Blake Street, St Mary Street, King Street, and a few others which have since changed vastly. They used to be rough cobble-stone streets and ill-kept roads, with a few dimly-lit lamps and lanterns. There were lumbering waggons and splendidly-equipped stage coaches. The principal hostelries were the *Swan*, the *George*, and the *King's Head*. There were two crosses in the town, one known as the High Cross on the Cornhill, the other was Pig Cross situated in the centre of Penel.

The town was governed by a Mayor, a Recorder, two Aldermen and 24 Councillors. Other officials were the Town Clerk, the Clerk of the Market, the Water Bailiff, two Sergeants-at-Mace, two Bailiffs, and a Receiver.

Holwell Cavern at Broomfield was discovered in 1800.

The Mayor was Mr Richard I. R. Jenkins.

1801 The population of Bridgwater was 3,634.

The Quaker's Meeting House was rebuilt.

A memorial stone was erected on the site of Athelney Abbey which had been founded by King Alfred.

The Mayor was Mr Robert Codrington.

1802 George Pocock and Jefferys Allen were elected M.P.s for Bridgwater.

The Mayor was Mr John Symes.

1803 Francis Egerton, the 3rd and last Duke of Bridgwater died and with him the Dukedom became extinct.

The Mayor was Mr Jacob Watson.

1804 At the General Election held on 26 June, John Hugglestone was elected M.P. for Bridgwater in the place of Jefferys Allen, who resigned.

The Mayor was Mr Robert Anstice.

1805 The Mayor was Mr Jefferys Allen.

1806 Vere Poulett and John Langston were elected M.P.s for Bridgwater.

The Mayor was Mr Richard I. R. Jenkins.

1807 At the General Election held on 5 May, George Pocock and William Thompson were elected M.P.s for Bridgwater.

Bridgwater gained the distinction of being the first town to petition Parliament to abolish the African slave trade in 1785. At the outset, little attention was paid to the Borough's plea, but many more similar appeals were made, and they contributed to the abolition of the slave trade in 1807.

The Mayor was Mr Charles H. Burt.

1808 The Mayor was Mr William Ford.

1809 At Bridgwater Assizes, Sarah Crocker, aged 22, was sentenced to death for stealing the sacramental plate from the Parish Church of Butcombe.

Alexander William Kinglake, the historian and author of the *History of the Crimean War,* was born at Taunton on 5 August. He was the eldest son of William, banker and solicitor of Taunton. He was elected Liberal M.P. for Bridgwater, together with Colonel Tynte, in 1857, and held his seat until 1868, when he was unseated upon petition and the Borough was disenfranchised.

The Mayor was Mr James Mills.

1810 A suggestion was made to cut a small canal between Bridgwater and Combwich Reach to allow quicker passage up and down the river and to enable large vessels which had to stop at Combwich to be brought into the port of Bridgwater. It was ultimately feared, however, that the toll which would be charged would not be sufficient to pay a reasonable rate of interest and the scheme was abandoned. In 1829 the scheme was revived, and though at a public meeting it unanimously agreed to, it was never carried out.

The Mayor was Mr. Thomas Symes.

1811 The population of the Town was 4,010

An Act was passed for making a navigable canal from Bristol to Taunton.

Henry J. Prince, the founder of the Agapemone at Spaxton, was born at Bath.

Durleigh Road did not then exist and Taunton Road did not extend beyond St Saviour's House. Neither St John's Church nor Holy Trinity Church had been built. There were no chapels apart from the Unitarian Church and the original building in which the Baptists worshipped.

The streets were not paved except by rude cobbles. There were no lamps, with the exception of two or three oil lanterns in the streets. The back streets were dark and filthy; food was dear, and not good and labour was scarce.

The Mayor was Mr Thomas Pyke.

1812 On 12 January John Jacob, afterwards the famous Brigadier-General, was born at the Vicarage House, Woolavington, near Bridgwater. He spent his early days in the neighbourhood of Bridgwater. His first military exploit was in connection with the Afghan War, and he soon afterwards rose to eminence in his profession. He had a distinguished career in the Honourable East India Company's Army, and eventually brought the rule of law and order to the wild country of the North West Frontier. When he died in 1858 the whole press of Great Britain were unanimous in their sympathetic obituaries to the memory of a brave and gallant soldier, and regarded his loss as a public calamity.

At the Election held on 7 October, George Pocock and William Astell were elected.

The Mayor was Mr William Inman.

1813 Bridgwater Races were again revived this year, although it was resolved that the races should be discontinued. The inhabitants of the town were determined to establish a racecourse. The races succeeded beyond all expectations and the immense concourse of respectable persons assembled on that occasion sufficiently attested the approving spirit that the undertaking would continue to elicit. Lieutenant-Colonel Tynte with characteristic spirit and judicious liberality presented a silver cup.

Bridgwater Hospital was established in this year. The Infirmary was opened in a house in Back Street (now Clare Street) at a rent of £35 a year, and £5 for a portion of the garden.

On Wednesday, 17 November, a great thunderstorm occurred at Bridgwater, damaging St Mary Church and spire. About half-past seven in the morning there was a violent storm of hail accompanied by a very heavy squall of wind from the north-west. The weather afterwards became dry and moderate at intervals, with occasional storms of rain and hail. At about half-past twelve some distant noise of thunder was heard and during the next quarter of an hour the thunder increased and some flashes of lightning were seen. The sky darkened dramatically and a heavy shower of rain started to fall. A very strong and explosive clap of thunder almost immediately followed and the spire and church were seriously damaged making it necessary to have extensive repairs carried out.

The Mayor was Mr James Mills.

1814 An advertisement appearing in a newspaper called the *Western Flying Post,* dated 24 February stated: 'To Builders, the Churchwardens of the Parish of Bridgwater, in the County of Somerset, hereby give notice that they will be ready to receive tenders, on or before the 25th of March next, for taking down and rebuilding 35 feet of the spire of the Church of the said Parish. In the meantime conditions of building, plans, sections and specifications of the same may be seen by application at the office of Mr. Trevor, Solicitor, at Bridgwater aforesaid'.

The Mayor was Mr William Ford.

1815 Repairs were carried out to the steeple of St Mary's Church which had been struck by lightning in 1813. The repairs were a difficult undertaking and it was on the advice of a nautical man that an ingenious method was at length agreed upon. Poles were hoisted to the top of the tower and two of them were lashed with strong ropes round the base of the steeple. Iron rings were riveted large enough to admit the ends of the other poles which were also lashed. Rope ladders were then fastened from pole to pole, and as one would mount the rigging of a vessel so the work was continued until the top steeple was reached. A crowd of people gathered to watch a celebrated pilot named Gover, who fearlessly mounted and brought down the weathercock. The repairs to the steeple were well executed by a local builder, Mr Thomas Hutchings, who constructed many other buildings in the town, including the Cornhill Buildings and the Dome.

The Mayor was Mr William Inman.

1816 A writer of the *Bristol Journal* suggested, as a plan to provide employment for some of the numerous poor who were in want of work, to make a grand inland navigation system to connect the Irish Sea through the Bristol Channel with the English Channel by a canal. This would open easy communication lines within the United Kingdom between North and South Wales, the counties of Monmouth and Hereford, and the River Severn with London and the intermediate parts; also with the eastern parts of the Kingdom, and westwards to Plymouth, and parts adjacent. There was no doubt that such a plan was practicable and it had been long in serious contemplation. The route proposed for it was from the celebrated bay in the Bristol Channel, called the Bay of Bridgwater, a little to the west of Steep Holme, and passing close to Bridgwater, Chard and Axminster, into the English Channel near Lyme Bay at Bridport.

Gin was 14s a gallon, cognac 25s 6d a gallon, and rum 18s 6d a gallon.

The original Wesleyan Chapel in King Street was built in 1816 and was restored and enlarged in 1860.

The Mayor was Mr William Inman.

1817 The Quantock Savings Bank was started at Nether Stowey in October, and it soon attained a position of influence in the neighbourhood. From a return in 1813 the funds amounted to £33,058; depositors were allowed interest rates of 3½ per cent per annum.

The Mayor was Mr Robert Anstice.

1818 At the Election held on 19 June, George Pocock and William Astell were elected.

In Somerset, cider was selling for 18s and £1 per hogshead from the Mill. In the shops apples were sold at the rate of 14 a penny.

The Mayor was Mr Jacob Watson.

1819 The Mayor was Mr John W. Crosse.

1820 At the General Election held on 7 March, William Astell (Liberal) and Charles K. Kemys-Tynte (Liberal) were elected.

This year appears to have been a period of distress in the town, probably owing to the hard winter, and the Masons were very liberal in voting a sum towards the alleviation of the hardships of the poor.

It was agreed to purchase a 'spacious house and garden' in Salmon Lane for £700 to enlarge the Infirmary. The Infirmary was then supported by voluntary contributions.

The Mayor was Mr Joseph R. Poole.

1821 A Turnpike Act was passed.

Sir George Pocock, ex-M.P. for Bridgwater was created a baronet.

Sir George Williams, the founder of the Young Men's Christian Association was born in Dulverton.

1821 There was only one person (a female) living in the county of Somerset, who had reached the age of 100 years. The number of inhabitants to a square mile in Somerset was 216. Whilst in Cornwall in was 194; in Devon 170; and in Dorset 144. Somerset was therefore more highly populated than the other three Western counties.

The population of the town was 6,155.

The Mayor was Mr Edward A. Stradling.

1822 It was estimated that the construction of a canal between Bridgwater and Taunton would cost £40,000.

There were unusual tides accompanied by severe rainstorms.

All roads leading into the town were repaired.

The coaching houses were the *Crown,* the *Angel,* the *Globe,* the *George* and the *London* inn.

A Congregational Church was built in Friarn Street.

The Mayor was Mr Richard Woodland.

1823 The proposed canal from Taunton to the River Parrett was intended to join it not far from the south side of the bridge at Bridgwater, which would render it safer for barges to enter the canal. The canal was expected to pay 10 per cent within three years.

The Mayor was Mr Thomas Symes.

1824 The *Royal Clarence* hotel was built on the site where formerly had stood *The Angel* and *The Crown.*

An Act was passed to amend the Act of 1811 and to change the name of the Bristol and Taunton Canal to the Bridgwater and Taunton Canal.

It was determined to proceed with the long-contemplated ship canal from Bridgwater to Bridport, by which ships of large burthen would navigate from the Bristol Channel to the English Channel without the delay of rounding Land's End.

A meeting of the subscribers to the intended improvements in Bridgwater took place, at which it was finally resolved that the designs of Mr. Carver, architect, for the erection of a superb Mansion House for the accommodation of the judges at the Assizes, a commodious hotel, and an elegant assembly and card room, should be erected.

The Trustees of the Bridgwater Turnpike Roads decided to construct a new line of road (on the Bristol branch) from Bridgwater to Pawlett, whereby one mile and a half would be saved and the steep hill at Puriton avoided. This, together with other improvements carried into effect by the Bristol and Bridgwater Trusts would reduce the distance between Bristol and Taunton by nearly four miles.

The Mayor was Mr Jonathan Toogood.

1825 A well-attended and highly respectable meeting was held at Wincanton to consider a plan to effect a railway from the River Parrett near Bridgwater to link up with the Basingstoke canal and collateral branches.

Numerous meetings were called in Bridgwater, Taunton, and generally throughout west Somerset and east Devon, for the purpose of constructing a grand ship canal, from a point at Stolford, on the Bristol Channel, towards Bridgwater, on to Creech, with a branch at Taunton, and ending at the town of Beer, on the English Channel. The celebrated Telford was appointed as engineer and most sanguine expectations were held as to the marvellous results to be accomplished. It was foretold that Taunton would become a 'second Liverpool'.

The Bridgwater and Taunton Canal, which is some fourteen miles in length, was cut. The opening ceremony took place in January 1827. Fourteen years later the canal was extended to Bridgwater Docks. The average width is 36ft. and the draught is 3ft. 6ins.

Bridgwater's first newspaper was established. It was called *The Bridgwater and Somersetshire Herald* and was printed and published by George Aubrey at Fore Street. It was a four-page newspaper, issued on Wednesdays, priced 7d.
It ceased with the issue of 3 August 1831 and was succeeded by a newspaper called *The Alfred* on 10 August 1831, a small eight-page journal printed on Mondays and also priced 7d.

The opening of the *Royal Clarence* hotel took place in July. At four o'clock 154 gentlemen assembled under the chairmanship of Mr R. Anstice, the Mayor, at a dinner to celebrate the opening. Four M.P.s and four clergymen were named among the company. The dinner, stated a report, 'was most sumptuously served, the wines were excellent, and every accommodation that possibly could be afforded to so large a party was most amply provided. The day passed off with the greatest conviviality. Some most delightful glees were sung, and everyone experienced a sincere pleasure in viewing the many public improvements in the town, of which the new and very handsome hotel wherein they were assembled exhibited one of the gratifying proofs'. The hotel took advertising space which stated 'R. Maynard takes leave, most respectfully, to inform the nobility, gentry and the public, that he has now entered upon the new hotel, which has been for some months fitting up in the most approved mode, and is now ready to receive company. The House is situated in the most eligible part of Bridgwater, is under the patronage of the principal inhabitants of the town and neighbourhood, and possesses every advantage for the reception of Noblemen and Gentlemen, travelling with their families; and also of Commercial and Agricultural gentlemen who are assured that the greatest exertions will be made to render this house in every respect particularly comfortable. Agricultural Gentlemen will find this house very convenient for the transaction of business, being immediately adjoining the new Markets. Excellent stabling, well-aired beds etc.—An ordinary every Thursday at half-past one.—Neat Landaus, Post Chariots, Chaises, a Hearse, Mourning Coaches'.

The Mayor was Mr Robert Anstice.

1826 The Market Hall Buildings and the Dome on the Cornhill were built by Mr Thomas Hutchings of Bridgwater.

A meeting of the inhabitants of Bridgwater was held at the *Mansion House* tavern, for the purpose of taking into consideration Mr Owen's plan for bettering the condition of the lower orders of society. The Hon Lionel Dawson was in the chair. The chairman stated to the meeting, at considerable length, the motives which had induced himself and other individuals to come forward on this occasion. The plan on which it was intended to proceed would be to raise a fund sufficient to purchase an estate, on which was to be built factories of different kinds. These factories, with the land, were to be let out to a community of the poorer class; and thus the agriculturists and mechanics would be able to work at their own callings, and the profits they made would be appropriated to the benefit of the community. Mr Tombs made some objections to the chairman's proposal, which were answered by a gentleman present. Mr Danger said that some means ought to be adopted to alleviate the condition of the poorer class of society but that he considered the present scheme entirely visionary as it would tend to bring all orders to a state of equality, which he thought could not subsist for a day. The chairman said he would remain for a short time in Bridgwater and would be happy to give any information in his power on the subject to those gentlemen who would call on him.

At the General Election held on 9 June, Mr William Astell (Liberal) and Mr Charles K. Kemys-Tynte (Liberal) were elected.

A newspaper called *The Bridgwater Herald* was first published.

The Mayor was Mr Edward Sealy.

1827 There had been outbreaks of ague in the neighbourhood of Taunton, and at Bridgwater and the marsh country of that district the number of cases were astonishingly great. It was all the more remarkable because of the absence of the disorder in that part of the country for nearly 10 years past and the predominance of typhus fever during the same period.

It was contemplated to form a Public Library in the town and the Trustees of the Market agreed to allow the new room over the Market House to be used for the purpose.

The Bridgwater and Taunton Canal was opened. The opening of the canal, together with the completion of railway links to Bristol, Taunton and Exeter in 1841-43 and improvements to the docks in 1841 stimulated commercial and industrial activity. At about this time the manufacture of bricks on a large scale was commenced; small ironworks were established, and Bridgwater prospered due to its ability to provide a complete range of building materials and household goods. The population increased considerably as workers migrated to the town from the surrounding rural areas. Between 1801 and 1832 the population rose from 3,600 to nearly 8,000 people.

The Mayor was Mr Richard Anstice.

1828 The Mayor was Mr Jacob Watson.

1829 In February of this year the Right Honourable Francis Henry, Earl of Bridgwater died. He left by his will the sum of £8,000 which paid for the compilation of works known as the *Bridgwater Treatises.*

The Mayor was Mr Frederick Axford.

1830 At the General Election held on 30 July, Mr William Astell (Liberal) and Mr Charles K. Kemys-Tynte (Liberal) were elected unopposed.

In 1830 there were pleas for increased Church accommodation which resulted, a few years later, in the building of Holy Trinity Church.

A visit to London in the 1830s by someone from Bridgwater was probably the one and only long journey he was likely to make in his life and he was looked upon as a townsman of some eminence. He would make the journey by stage coach, setting off from the Cornhill. The coach travelled via *Piper's* inn, through Glastonbury, Shepton Mallet, Frome, Warminster and Andover. Here, in the little Hampshire town, passengers changed into another coach for completion of the journey which took exactly 13 hours and was a very pleasant and interesting trip.

Such was the importance in one's life of a visit to London, that some people contemplating undertaking the journey were advised by their lawyers to have their wills drawn up and signed before leaving Bridgwater! One townsman, it is recorded, even had a hot bath on the night before he set out so that in the event of an accident he might 'make a clean corpse'.

In those days Bridgwater was well served by stage coaches not only travelling to London, but also to other cities and large towns. Coaching inns and posting houses were busy by day and night. Shops and street stalls were open too, even on Sundays. In the High Street there were butchers' stalls which were open on Sundays until the bells of St Mary's Church ceased to ring out for morning service; but long before that hour Bridgwater's best-known stage coach *Swiftsure* had left the town and was on its daily run to London.

Swiftsure was the pride of the town. It was well horsed and well equipped within and without. It was quite an event to see it depart and to welcome its return the next evening. The coach left the *Royal Clarence* hotel for London every Monday, Wednesday and Friday at 7.30 a.m., and arrived at Holborn, London at 9 p.m. the same night.

A General Meeting of Merchants, Shipowners and others interested in the improvement of the port and harbour of Bridgwater was held to consider the propriety of applying to Parliament for a Bill to carry into effect the plan proposed by Mr Jessop to improve the port of Bridgwater. Mr Jessop suggested that the port be made into a floating harbour, and that with canals for ships and barges, the port would become more accessible than it was then. V. Stuckey Esq. was called to the chair and after several gentlemen had delivered their sentiments on the occasion, it was resolved that Mr Jessop's plan was well calculated to accomplish the ends in view, and ought forthwith to be carried into effect. The chairman at once entered his name for 20 shares in the undertaking, the estimated expense of which was somewhat above £100,000; the work to be completed in about three years. The meeting adopted the following resolutions as the basis of their proceedings:

'That the trade of the Port of Bridgwater had been regularly increasing for many years past, at the rate of about 5,000 tons registered measure per annum, the same having in the year 1822 amounted to above 75,000 tons, and in the year ending in October 1829, to above 112,000 tons, and that causes are now in operation, and others are likely soon to be brought into action, by which it may reasonably be expected that the trade will in future years be augmented in a still more rapid progression. That the port of Bridgwater, and the accommodations which it affords are altogether inadequate to the existing state of its trade, and that great delay, loss of time, and danger often arises to vessels frequenting the same, for the want of sufficient quay-room, from their being left dry during the reflux of the tides, from the circuitous course of the river, and from the water during neap-tides, not being deep enough to float vessels up to the quay at Bridgwater, in consequence of which commerce is much checked, and many advantages are lost to capital and industry, not only of the town and neighbourhood, but of other large and populous towns and districts connected therewith.'

The Mayor was Mr William J. Allen.

1831 At the General Election held on 30 April, Colonel Charles K. Kemys-Tynte (Liberal) and Mr William Astell (Liberal) were elected. The result was:

Colonel Charles K. Kemys-Tynte (Liberal)	337
Mr William Astell (Liberal)	213
Mr Henry Shirley (Conservative)	202

James Knight, a shoemaker of Spaxton, drank 11 glasses of gin for a wager, at Pawlett, and died immediately after from the effects.

A gunpowder explosion occurred at the shop of a man named Bennett, in St Mary Street and wrecked it. Much damage was done and a public subscription was made for the proprietor.

The population of the town was 7,807.

A newspaper called *The Alfred, London Weekly Journal, and Bridgwater and Somersetshire General Advertiser* was established on Monday, 10 August, by John Bowen, who was a retired engineer and who had made his fortune in India. He ran his own newspaper so that he could air his opinions freely. He was 'a live wire' and was of a somewhat truculent disposition. At the time of the Reform Bill his reactionary political opinions roused the anger of a mob who wrecked his house and knocked him senseless; the Riot Act was read during this violent fracas. His newspaper succeeded *The Bridgwater and Somersetshire Herald.* It was priced 7d. and was partially printed in London. The editor was Harry Clement Heard, and it had offices in St Mary Street. It ceased with the issue of 30 December 1833 and was incorporated in *The Dorset County Chronicle and Somerset Gazette* on 2 January 1834.

At a public meeting of the inhabitants of Bridgwater, held at the *Bristol Arms* inn, under the presidency of the Mayor, John Evered (who opened the business of the day by a very able appeal to the electors) it was resolved to establish a Political Union, for the purpose of 'promoting purity of election, and of prosecuting and destroying, by all legal means, bribery and corruption'. B. Lovibond followed the Mayor and after an excellent speech, read the rules and articles which were seconded by Mr Brown and carried unanimously. Nearly 200 voters immediately subscribed their names and cash.

Three hundred and sixty people, principally labourers and mechanics, among whom were many entire families, sailed from Bridgwater in two vessels, the *Friends* and the *Euphrosyne,* as emigrants for Canada. Nearly one hundred of them were sent out at the expense of the Marquis of Bath.

An Election Notice printed on behalf of Mr C. K. K. Tynte, read as follows:

'To the Truly Free and Independent Electors of the Borough of Bridgwater: Gentlemen and Friends, the Triumphant manner in which you have this day done me the honour of returning me for a Fourth Time to Parliament, by the Pure and Independent exercise of your unsolicited votes, you may well suppose renders it difficult for me to find words sufficiently strong to express my deep sense of gratitude for the continuance of your unbounded confidence and attachment. It is natural that I should feel increased obligation to you, on every fresh occasion that you have done me the honour of calling upon me to represent you: in the present instance, your kindness and consideration towards me far surpass those of any former one, and is (if possible) still more fully appreciated by me. At this time of general excitement throughout the Kingdom, and with the great question of Reform before you, you have placed me at the Head of the Poll by an unprecedented and proud majority, without requiring me to solicit a Single Vote, or to make a Pledge of any kind. The unceasing exertions of the

Committee, and the zeal of those True and Faithful Friends who have done me the honour to vote for me, rendered my taking any part in the arrangement of the Election perfectly unnecessary, I have, therefore, had only to obey your wishes in standing forward under your favour, to support those principles which we mutually profess. Returned again to Parliament in this constitutional, independent, and honourable manner, I shall endeavour to discharge my future duties in such a manner as may (to the best of my judgement) tend to the honour and dignity of the Crown, the support of the Constitution, and the general benefit of fellow subjects of all descriptions, and of your own Local interests in particular. I shall take as early a time for returning you my personal thanks, as other circumstances attending a General Election will allow me. In the meantime, I remain, Gentlemen, With the most sincere Respect, Esteem and Obligation, Your most Grateful Faithful, and Attached Friend, C. K. K. Tynte. Halswell, May 2nd, 1831. Awbrey, Printer, Herald Office, Bridgwater.'

The Mayor was Mr John Evered.

1832 The Quarter Sessions for the borough and parish were held at the Town Hall on 7 January.

A man was sentenced to one years' imprisonment with hard labour for stealing a £5 promissory note and two sovereigns. A woman was sentenced to three months' hard labour for stealing a handkerchief and a sovereign and a half. A man was sentenced to be 'once whipped' and a months' imprisonment for the theft of a piece of oak timber.

A red-ware pottery was established in Salmon Lane by Mr Jeboult of Taunton. He had just moved out of 'the glass cone' which he had occupied for about a year.

At the General Election held on 11 December the candidates were:

Colonel Charles K. Kemys-Tynte (Liberal).
Mr William Tayleur (Liberal).
Mr Chatteris (Conservative).
Mr Twiss (Conservative).

Colonel K. Kemys-Tynte and Mr William Tayleur were elected. Mr Chatteris and Mr Twiss withdrew.

A large number of people emigrated to Quebec, Canada, from Bridgwater. A local newspaper contained the following advertisement:

'Direct from Quebec. The Fine Fast Sailing copper fastened ship *Euphrosyne,* burthen 500 tons, Joseph Sampson, Master, will positively sail from Bridgwater, the beginning of August 1832, wind and weather permitting. The above vessel is 6ft. high between decks, and will be fitted up for the comfort and accommodation of Passengers, which will offer an eligible opportunity for Emigrants to settle in Upper Canada. Rate of Passage, Cabin Passengers £12; Steerage ditto £3 5s. 0d., and find themselves; children under fourteen years of age £2 5s. 0d.; under seven years £1 5s. 0d.; children at the breast free. For Freight or Passage apply to Captain Joseph Sampson, North Gate, Bridgwater, or to Mr. Thomas Sully, Ship Agent, if by letter, post paid.'

On Monday, 24 September, the members of the Bridgwater Cricket Club held their first Annual Dinner at the Grand Jury Room, when several of the neighbouring gentry were present. About fifty persons sat down to an excellent dinner. After an evening spent in well regulated harmony, the company separated to resume next season this manly and innocent amusement which has been encouraged by the highest dignatories of the kingdom, not only by their precept but by their example.

A notice in connection with St Matthew's Fair in this year read as follows:

'Notice is hereby given that this Fair will be held at Bridgwater, as usual, on the 2nd, 3rd and 4th days of October next but it having been represented to the Magistrates by the Board of Health that they are apprehensive of the Disease called Cholera, which the Town is providentially exempt, may be communicated with the inhabitants by Vagrants, and other Idle and Disorderly Persons. Notice is hereby further given, that the Magistrates have appointed an additional number of Constables, who, in conjunction with the regular Constables, have strict orders to apprehend and bring before them, all Vagrants and other idle and Disorderly Persons, who shall resort to the said Fair, in order that they may be dealt with according to the law. By order of the Magistrates. Trevor, Town Clerk. Bridgwater. 24th September, 1832.'

The following report in a local newspaper, *The Alfred,* of the Fair gives an indication of the importance of the event from a business point of view:

'A greater quantity of cheese was pitched for sale than has been known for a number of years, the sale of which was rather dull in the early part of the morning, but towards the close of the day nearly the whole was disposed of at the following prices:

Best from 50s. to 60s.;
Seconds from 50s. to 56s.; and
Inferior from 25s. to 28s. per cwt.

Bacon from 6d. to 6½d. per lb. The supply of books and shoes was immense. There were at least a hundred standings of shoe makers, this being the great mart for these articles, and probably a greater stock was exhibited for sale here than at any other Fair in the West of England. The weather being remarkably fine, the company on the second day, which may be called the pleasure fair, might have been compared to a rapid and overflowing tide, so that from the continual influx of people into the Town it might have been thought that the whole population of Somersetshire had been congregated at Bridgwater. The scarcity of money was universally complained of and this, added to the amazing supply of every article both of live and dead stock at high prices could not be looked for except the article wanted was of first rate quality.'

The Mayor was Mr Joseph Ruscombe Poole.

1833 Wednesday, 16 January was observed in the town as a day of solemn thanksgiving, as Bridgwater had happily been spared the ravages of cholera which had caused such heavy mortality in other places. Towards the end of the year, smallpox broke out and about forty deaths occurred through it.

The Mayor was Mr Richard Anstice.

1834 The Gas Works in Old Taunton Road was established and started this year and was the property of shareholders. The street lamps in Bridgwater were first lit with gas on 22 May and the first gas lamp to be lit in business premises was in the establishment of Edward Jefferies, Chemist, Fore Street. The Theatre, situated in Back Street, now Clare Street, on the site which was Theatre Place, was one of the first public buildings in which this lighting was used.

The Mayor was Mr Richard Woodland.

1835 The floating dock, basin and harbour, which would connect the Bridgwater and Taunton Canal and afford accommodation to a large number of vessels, and provide a considerable line of wharfage was started in this year. Mr John W. Ford laid the foundation stone of the docks.

At the General Election held on 5 January, Colonel Charles K. Kemys-Tynte (Liberal) and Mr John Temple.Leader (Liberal) were elected.The results were:

Colonel Charles K. Kemys-Tynte (Liberal)	234
Mr John Temple Leader (Liberal)	208
Mr. Henry Broadwood (Conservative)	190
Mr Martin (Conservative)	162

The Parliamentary Election cost nearly £30,000.

A ship canal from Bridgwater to Combwich was proposed.

The Municipal Corporation Act was passed. On Christmas Day the old Corporation met at the house of the Mayor, Mr Anthony Southby, and walked to church for the last time under the old régime. The Corporation then comprised the Mayor, two Aldermen and 21 Burgesses, none of whom were tradesmen, but gentlemen, and had to attest that they had taken the sacrament. On a Sunday early in January when the Act came into force, the newly-constituted Corporation met at the Town Hall and went to church in state, amid much excitement. The procession was headed by Webb, the bellman, in a new scarlet coat, knee breeches and cocked hat. The invitations were generally extended, first to odd members of the Corporation and later on to the principal residents and tradesmen.

The Mayor was Mr Anthony Southby.

1836 On 19 August the first Temperance Meeting ever held in Bridgwater took place at the Friend's Meeting House in Friarn Street. These meetings were held by James Teare and at first the movement received some scant sympathy. At almost every meeting some disturbance took place—the forms and chairs were repeatedly broken up and on more than one occasion the pieces were hurled at the speakers and occupants on the platform.

The Bristol and Exeter Railway Act was passed; the railway came to Bridgwater in 1841, to Taunton in 1842, and to Exeter in 1843.

An Act was passed for making a navigable canal from the River Parrett to Barrington.

The Mayor was Mr Thomas W. Inman.

1837 The Baptist Chapel in St Mary Street was rebuilt; it was founded in the 17th century. There is seating for 710 persons.

A Parliamentary By-Election was held on 16 May and the result was as follows:

Mr Henry Broadwood (Conservative)	279
Mr Richard Brinsley Sheriden (Liberal)	221

Mr Henry Broadwood was elected with a majority of 58 votes.

At the General Election held on 26 July the result was as follows:

Mr Henry Broadwood (Conservative)	280
Mr Philip Courtenay (Conservative)	278
Sir T. B. Lethbridge (Liberal)	5
Mr Richard Brinsley Sheriden (Liberal)	2

Mr Broadwood and Mr Courtenay were elected.

A fire was discovered in the Pottery occupied by Mr Jeboult in Salmon Lane. The engines arrived quickly and the destructive element was soon got under control, but not before the whole of the interior of the premises, with a large quantity of earthenware, was destroyed.

There came to work at a drapery store in the Town, a 16-year-old apprentice, George Williams, who was destined to become the founder of the Y.M.C.A.

The 28 June, being the Coronation day of Queen Victoria, was kept as a general holiday with much rejoicing. The Corporation and Freemasons walked to St Mary's Church and afterwards went in procession through the streets of the town.

In September a 'Bridgwater Guardian Association' was established, which had for its object 'the protection of persons and property from felons and other offenders'. To attain this object a committee was empowered to offer rewards for information leading to the conviction of offenders against the person or property of any of the members. The rewards varied between £5 and £15 according to the offence.

The Mariners' Congregational Church in St John Street was built in this year. It was designed originally for the use of seamen connected with the port. It seated about 350 persons.

The following cutting from a Somerset newspaper regarding St Mary's Church in February of this year is of interest; it reads as follows:

'A Committee of the respectable inhabitants of this Town has for some time been engaged in ascertaining to how great an extent the sittings in our Parish Church may be enlarged, so as to afford greater accommodation to the increasing population, and on Saturday, at a public meeting of the inhabitants the Committee made their report, when it was resolved that 600 additional sittings should be erected. The population of the Town at the present time is about 7,300 and on completion of the intended alterations 1,600 persons will be supplied with sittings in the Church. It is computed that the dissenting places of worship offer room for 2,500, leaving a total of 3,600 persons who are entirely deprived of the means of attending Public Divine Worship'.

An Election Notice printed on behalf of Mr Richard Brinsley Sheriden read as follows:

'To the Worthy and Independent Electors of the Borough of Bridgwater. Gentlemen, Having completed my canvas, I beg leave to return you my most grateful thanks, for the kind and flattering reception you have given me, and for the numerous and voluntary promises of support which I have received. Before presenting myself to your notice, I knew that the Reformers of Bridgwater had, for two successive Parliaments, elected Liberal Representatives; encouraged by this fact, I ventured to solicit your suffrages, and the entire success of my canvas has determined me to adhere to your cause. If, during my canvas, I have omitted to call upon any Elector, I beg that it may be attributed to accident, and not to any want of respect. It now only remains for me publicly and solemnly to declare my intention to appear on the Hustings, in order that every Elector of Bridgwater may have an opportunity of recording his Vote, and ascertaining his political Principles and Independence. I have the honour to be, Gentlemen, your obliged and faithful servant. Richard Brinsley Sheriden. Bridgwater, 9th May, 1847, Whitby, Printer, Cornhill, Bridgwater.'

The Mayor was Mr Robert Ford.

1838 Dinner was cooked on the ice-covered river.

The Mayor was Mr Richard Woodland.

1839 The Holy Trinity Church, Taunton Road, was built of stone with a belfry containing one bell. Its interior was surrounded by a gallery.

The Coaching Houses were the *Royal Clarence,* the *Albion,* the *George,* the *Rose and Crown,* the *Bristol Arms,* the *Globe* and the *New* inn.

The Mayor was Mr Thomas Symes.

1840 The River Parrett divided the town into two parts which were connected by an elegant iron bridge. The west part of the town was the largest and most respectable—the streets were well paved and lighted with gas, and some of the shops were very handsome. Some houses were built of brick and some of stone. The portion of the town on the other side of the river was called Eastover. The Town Hall and Court House was a substantial and convenient building containing Council Rooms, an Assize Court, and adjoining it were convenient lodgings for the judges.

The river was navigable to Bridgwater for vessels of 300 tons. A great many barges conveyed goods to Langport. Inland from Bridgwater the river was navigable for barges to Taunton and was there connected by a branch with the Grand Western Canal. A new cut was in progress for carrying the Taunton Canal to the river on the north of the town, which would be very convenient for traders. The floating dock at the junction of the new canal and river was nearly completed and would be of sufficient magnitude to contain shipping of a large size which promised to be of immense value to the port, and indirectly to the whole of west Somerset. A steam tug had just recently been placed upon the river which helped traders considerably.

The number of registered electors for the Borough was 570 and the town returned two members to parliament. The chief place of public resort in the neighbourhood of Bridgwater was Halswell, the seat of Colonel Tynte; the grounds surrounding were very beautiful, and most kindly opened to the public by the generous proprietor.

The Public Offices were the Custom House on the quay, the Post Office in Victoria Street; the Registry Office in Chilton Road; the Excise Office at the *Lamb* inn, High Street; the Savings Bank in High Street; the Stamp Office in Friarn Street; the Registry of births, etc. in Dampiet Street; Public Officers were the Recorder; the Town Clerk; the Treasurer; the Clerk of the Peace; the Coroner; the Parish Clerk; the Collector (Custom House); the Comptroller of Customs; the Surgeon to the Union; the Clerk to the Union; the Governor of the Workhouse; the Clerk to the Commissioner of Taxes; the Clerk to the Magistrates; the Supervisor of Excise; the Excise Man; the Land Waiter; and the Sheriff's Officer.

The places of worship were the Parish Church of St Mary's; the Independent Congregational Church in Friarn Street; the Unitarian Chapel in Dampiet Street; the Baptist Chapel in St Mary Street; the Wesleyan Chapel in Dampiet Street; the Mariners' Congregational Church in St John Street; the Irvingites Chapel in Dampiet Street; and the Friends' Meeting House in Friarn Street.

The Girls' National School was in the Crescent; Dr Morgan's School at the Mount; and the British and Foreign School at the Mount.

There was an Eye Infirmary in Victoria Street; an Infirmary in Salmon Lane; and a literary and scientific Institution at the Market Hall, Cornhill. There were six Academies for boys and girls day and boarding schools; one architect; three banks which were Edward and John Sealey's Bridgwater Bank at the Quay; Stuckey's Banking Company on the Cornhill; and the West of England and South Wales District Bank on the Cornhill.

There were 21 bakers, 2 barristers, 2 basket-makers, 8 blacksmiths, 1 block-maker, 29 boot and shoe makers, 4 booksellers, 2 braziers, 18 butchers, 11 cabinet makers, 13 carpenters, 4 carriers, 1 carver and guilder, 2 chandlers, 5 cheese-makers, 6 chemists and druggists, 5 clock- and watch-makers, 2 clothes-men, 4 coachmakers, 2 coach proprietors, 4 coal merchants, 6 coffee and eating houses, 4 confectioners, 1 conveyancer, 3 coopers, 9 corn factors, 2 curriers, 2 cutlers, 14 drapers, 2 dyers, 2 follmongers, 2 fruiterers, 3 glass and china sellers, 1 glover, 33 grocers, 1 gun-maker, 6 hairdressers, 3 hatters, 3 estate agents, 63 inns and public houses, of which the following are now not in existence:

The Albion, St Mary Street
The Angel, St Mary Street
The Anchor, West Quay
The Baker's Arms, Barclay Street
The Bull and Butcher, No 26 High Street
The Cheese House, St Mary Street
The Cottage Inn, Back Street
The Castle Inn, Binford Place

The Crown and Sceptre, West Street
The Devonshire Arms, Friarn Street
The Dove, West Street
The George Hotel, George Lane
The Globe Hotel, Eastover
The Half Moon, Monmouth Street
The Halswell House, West Street
The Horse Keeper's Return, St Mary Street
The Lamb, No 14 High Street (now *The Duke of Monmouth*)
The London Inn, Eastover
The Marquess of Wellington, St Mary Street
The Mason's Arms, Penel Orlieu
The Moulder's Arms, Barclay Street
The Nag's Head, West Street
The New Inn, Eastover
The Old Oak, No 31 High Street
The Parrett, Victoria Street
The Plume of Feathers, St Mary Street
The Pilot Boat, Salmon Lane
The Ploughboy, West Street
The Queen's Head Eastover
The Rising Sun, Friarn Street
The Ship and Castle Inn, Fore Street
Star Inn, Eastover
The Three Tuns Inn, Penel Orlieu
The Ring of Bells, Back Lane
The Railroad, Eastover
The Seven Stars, Friarn Street
The Three Queens, St John Street
The Victoria Inn, West Street
The White Horse Inn, St Mary Street
The William IV, Back Lane
The Whale Inn, Salmon Lane

There were 4 ironmongers, 1 land surveyor, 1 laundress, 2 law stationers, 8 maltsters, 5 masons, 5 merchants, 7 milliners and dress makers, 7 ministers of religion, 3 professors of music, 2 nurserymen and seedsmen, 9 painters, glaziers and plumbers, 1 patten maker, 2 pawnbrokers, 1 plasterer, 5 printers, 4 rope-makers, 6 sadlers, 2 sail-makers, 2 ship brokers, 1 ship builder, 2 shipwrights, 3 silversmiths, 4 stonemasons, 8 straw bonnet makers, 10 surgeons, 22 tailors, 1 tanner, 2 tea dealers, 2 thatchers, 2 timber merchants, 1 toy warehouse, 1 turner, 3 upholsterers, 1 veterinary surgeon, 1 wheelwright, 2 white smiths, 4 wine merchants, 1 worsted manufacturer.

The old 'Pig Cross' at Penel Orlieu was removed.

Mr Jeboult's Pottery was removed.

Sir George Pocock, M.P. for Bridgwater for over 22 years, died.

There was a fire when two houses opposite the Market Hall and Dome on the Cornhill were burnt to the ground; fortunately there was no loss of life.

The Mayor was Mr Frederick Axford.

1841 At the General Election held on 29 June, Mr Henry Broadwood (Conservative) and Mr Thomas Seaton Foreman (Conservative) were elected. The result was as follows:

Mr Henry Broadwood (Conservative)	280
Mr Thomas Seaton Foreman (Conservative)	276
Mr Edward Simcoe Drewe (Liberal)	247
Mr Augustine Robinson (Liberal)	242

On 25 March a great development was celebrated in Bridgwater when the docks were opened.

This year was important in the history of Bridgwater as the town was connected with Bristol by the Bristol and Exeter Railway, though the route to Exeter still awaited completion.

The *Railway* hotel was built and was popular with travellers. The Liberal candidates at elections sometimes made it their temporary residence when visiting the town.

The population of the town was 10,430.

The Mayor was Mr R. Bagehot.

1843 The Mayor was Mr W. D. Bath.

1844 The financial statement for the year ending 31 August, issued by the Borough Treasurer of the town, Mr William Jones, revealed some interesting facts of income and expenditure. Total receipts for the year totalled £3,260 17s. 8¾d. In 1844 Borough rates brought in £332 13s. 11d.; rents and tolls £454 162. 4d.; sale of land £1,657; and fines £1 10s. 0d. The sum of £343 19s. 11d. was paid in salaries, pensions and allowances to the municipal officers; £421 5s. 11d. to police constables and the gaol. Maintenance of prisoners cost £161 9s. 4d. The amount of £110 13s. 6d. was paid for the administration of justice, prosecutions etc. The Coroner received £22 15s. 8d., and the sum of £54 3s. 11d. was put towards public works and repair of buildings. The Treasurer's account was signed as being correct on 27 September 1844 by John Ruddock (Mayor's Auditor), John Whitby, and John Trevor (Borough Auditors).

The Mayor was Mr T. H. Watson.

1845 A Horse Tramway was constructed by the Bridgwater Corporation which ran from Bridgwater station to a wharf on the River Parrett.

The Agapemone was founded at Spaxton by the Rev Henry James Prince.

An Act was passed to improve the navigation of the river.

The Mayor was Mr J. Ruddock.

1846 On Thursday, 1 January, a newspaper called *The Bridgwater Times* was established by Mr Samuel Bowditch in Fore Street. It was a small eight-page weekly, priced 5d. It had an average circulation of 1,200, and this increased when the price was reduced to 3½d. It ceased on 11 September 1861.

St John the Baptist's Church in Blake Place, Eastover, was erected by the Rev John Moore Capes, M.A. of Shipton-Moyne, and consecrated on 17 August.

A Roman Catholic Church was built in Gardon Terrace. In 1882 it was superseded by the Church of St Joseph in Binford Place.

The Mayor was Mr John Sealy.

1847 An Election Notice was printed on behalf of Mr Henry Broadwood and read as follows:

'To the Worthy and Independent Electors of the Borough of Bridgwater. Gentlemen, the approaching Dissolution of Parliament renders it necessary that I should formerly announce to you my intention of soliciting a renewal of the honourable and important Trust which you have been pleased to confide in me in three successive Parliaments, during which I have endeavoured, to the best of my ability, to discharge its duties with assiduity and faithfulness. My general principles are well known to you, I will therefore only say that I am ready and willing to entertain and co-operate in every well considered measure of social improvement. The repeal of the protective duties on Corn has now become the law of the Land, and I trust that measure will tend to the benefit of all classes. It ever has been and always will be a source of pride and gratification to me to attend to the local interests of your Borough. I shall have the pleasure of paying my respects, personally, to the Electors without delay. I have the honour to be, Gentlemen, Your Faithful and Obliged Servant, Henry Broadwood, 5 Whitehall Yard, London, July 22nd, 1847. F. G. Dowty, Printer, Bridgwater.'

At the General Election held 29 July, Colonel K. Kemys-Tynte (Liberal) and Mr Henry Broadwood (Conservative) were elected. The result was as follows:

Colonel K. Kemys-Tynte (Liberal)	395
Mr Henry Broadwood (Conservative)	265
Mr Sergeant Gazelee (Liberal)	196

The Mayor was Mr John C. Parker.

1848 Bridgwater generally had some excellent streets, containing many handsome buildings; the streets were well paved, lighted with gas, and kept remarkably clean; water was obtained from wells sunk for that purpose. The Docks had been opened seven years previously and a new harbour at Dunball was opened in 1843. There was a handsome and commodious Market House, nearly half an acre in extent; an attractive circular portico under which the Corn Market was held, while other parts of the building were appropriated to butchers, fruiterers, greengrocers, fishmongers and poulterers, who catered most liberally and successfully for the public taste.

There were regular sailing services from the Docks, the most outstanding being the ship *Ottowa* owned by Messrs Stuckey & Bagehot, which left every March and August for Quebec. There were regular services all the year round to Dublin, Swansea, Cardiff and Liverpool. Horse-drawn coaches, omnibus services, and carrier services plied between most surrounding villages, and Sutton's omnibus from the *Royal Clarence* hotel met every train. John Bletchley plied a carrier service between St John Street, Bridgwater and Farringdon Street, London; and Elisha Hallett from the *Ship Aground,* Eastover, to Burnham-on-Sea and intermediate places.

The Mayor was Mr James Trevor.

1849 A great number of needed improvements were carried out to the Bridgwater Infirmary at a cost of £428. In the same year an outbreak of cholera in the town severely tested the resources of the Institution, and over 1,000 patients were treated during the outbreak.

The defective sanitary arrangements and impure water are believed to have caused the visitation. The Corporation and townspeople formed themselves into a kind of 'vigilance committee' and visited all the lanes and by-places, routing out all the nuisances. Strict rules were also enforced as to the admission of strangers into the town and citizens who wished to leave Bridgwater on any pretext were obliged to be furnished with passes by the Mayor, which were not forthcoming if the applicant had resided in a cholera-stricken house. Before the dreadful disease was eradicated over 200 people died. Of this number 88 died in Eastover, and were buried in an isolated spot in St John's Churchyard, where a stone bore the following inscription:

In memory of the decease of 88 persons from
Cholera, 1840. From plague, pestilence and a
sudden death; good Lord, deliver us.

The Mayor was Mr James Haviland.

1850 A skittles match between a local team and one from Southampton was played at Mr Woolferson's Brewery, St Mary Street. It lasted from 10 a.m. to 10 p.m., and only five minutes was allowed for refreshments. A Mr Ireland was declared the winner and received the sum of £14.

The Mayor of Bridgwater, Mr Robert Ford, had to read the Riot Act on the occasion of festivities at Bridgwater. Some farmers were assembled at the *White Hart* hotel, and being excited began to throw the balls and pins from the skittle alley out of the window at the crowd. The latter retorted, returning the balls with a good deal of vehemence and smashing the windows to atoms. A most uproarious scene ensued, and the few constables present were utterly unable to quell the storm. This scene, however, was the outcome of severe political feeling, which was ever to assert itself upon the most trivial occasions. Within the *White Hart* hotel it was alleged, were the Tories; outside were the Whigs. This, of course, explained everything. Politics in those days were useful in providing amusement as well as instruction. They exonerated all excess, and condoned all violence.

1851 The Penny Bank was formed, and the Committee of the object met for the first time at Mr Hookin's *Temperance* hotel, Angel Crescent, on a Monday evening to receive the names and money of those who wanted to become depositors. At the close of the evening it was ascertained that the sum of £3 10s. 6d. had been paid in by 109 subscribers, varying from a penny upwards. The Committee continued to meet at the *Temperance* hotel every Monday evening for the purpose of receiving subscriptions and enrolling new members.

On 16 June the Bridgwater Steam Towing Company's steamer *Perseverance* made a pleasure trip to Minehead. This trip originated at the suggestion of several gentleman of the town, and also in the desire of the Towing Company to give their townsmen the opportunity to enjoy a trip down the Channel. The pleasure of the party was greatly enhanced by the presence of a good portion of the fair townswomen. Arriving off Minehead the company went ashore for between two and three hours and enjoyed a ramble over the hills in the neighbourhood which commands some highly interesting and romantic scenery.

On the return trip the lady of the Rev J. C. Collins presided at a temporarily fitted-up tea-table and, assisted by several gentlemen, teas were handed to every lady on board, a kindly act, duly and gratefully appreciated. A band enlivened the hours with the performance of a variety of airs and added much to the enjoyment of the holiday. It was the intention of the owners of the steamer to send her out on similar excursions once or twice a fortnight during the summer season, and that the Mayor and Corporation might set aside a day from the arduous toils of local government to breathe the refreshing sea breeze on the *Perseverance*. However, all enjoyed themselves right pleasantly, except for a few who, looking at the mighty deep, became qualmish and confined the secrets of their bosoms to its depths.

On Monday, 19 June, a pleasure trip was made by the steamer *Cardiff Castle* to Flat Holme. More than 150 pleasure-seekers were on board, among them a number of the gentler sex, some with children. The weather was windy and the sea rough and when sailing down the Channel to get around the Gore, the deck was washed by each successive wave and the majority were drenched to the skin. The after part of the vessel was crowded and the deck covered with the sick and the helpless of both sexes. Arriving at Flat Holme, 31 people went ashore. Almost immediately the wind, which had before blown stiffly from the north-west, increased, and the sea became rougher so that the steamer was obliged to make for Cardiff for shelter. The pleasure-seekers were consequently left on Flat Holme until the following morning, without beds, and many of them on 'short commons', not anticipating such a Robinson Crusoe-like event on a desolate island. The next day proved, for a good number, a day of fast and they were left to contemplate the joy of returning home as many had done the day before. The steamer returned on Tuesday after having left the river at Bridgwater on Monday morning. It was suggested that females who were fond of these steamer excursions should never take their children with them; if they are unwell they become a burden to others, and under the most favourable circumstances are an annoyance to the Company.

It was agreed by the Bridgwater Corporation that tenders whould be obtained for the repair and winding-up of St Mary's Church Parish clock. Two tenders were received by the churchwardens, one of them from Mr W. Cockings sen. offering to do the small piece of service for the parish for the modest little sum of £70! The other tender was Mr James Rich, who offered to do the same service for £15, thus turning the chimes in accordance with parish feelings. The churchwardens considered that the latter gentleman 'richly' deserved the tender.

The Bridgwater Agricultural Association held its first Show at Blacklands in the town. The President was Colonel Charles K. Kemys-Tynte, M.P. for Bridgwater, the Secretary Mr A. C. Heard, the Treasurer Mr Richard Woodland, and the Mayor Robert Fort Esq.

The population of the town was 10,883.

St Mary's Churchyard was closed for burial purposes and a new cemetery was consecrated in Wembdon Road, by the Bishop of Jamaica on 10 September.

Good nature was abused by the attempt of certain people in Bridgwater to palm themselves off as press reporters at public exhibitions or at lectures in order to obtain free admission to these events. The *Bridgwater Times* stated that these people should not be recognised and that their names should be published if this abuse persisted.

In November, the 10th Annual Dinner of the Saltlands Bowling Society took place at the *Royal Clarence* hotel, under the presidency of Mr W. J. Knight who was ably supported by vice-chairman Mr Edwin Down. About thirty gentlemen sat down; the dinner was served in Mr and Mrs Sutton's superior style, and the wines were of a recherché description. After the usual loyal and patriotic toasts were given from the chair, a number of glees, rounds and songs were exceedingly well sung. The Society enjoyed a 'right merrie' meeting and did not part until late. During dinner the company were enlivened with some very excellent music from the Weston-Super-Mare Sax-Horn Band.

1852 At the General Election held on 7 July, Colonel C. K. Kemys-Tynte (Liberal) and Mr Brent Spencer Follett (Conservative) were elected. The result was as follows:

Colonel C. K. Kemys-Tynte (Liberal)	272
Mr Brent Spencer Follett (Conservative)	244
John Christopher Mansell (Conservative)	177
Lord Henley (Liberal)	149
Mr Alexander William Kinglake (Liberal)	101

A large number of persons from Bridgwater emigrated to New York.

The 18 November was the funeral of the Duke of Wellington, and all the shops in the town were closed and business generally suspended.

A very handsome stained glass window in the Corporation Chapel of St Mary's Church was presented by Mr Thomas Ford, Mayor of Bridgwater.

St Matthew's Fair commenced on a Saturday early in October and was ushered in with as glorious a morning as ever broke. The field was covered with booths, shows and standings, the owners of which were in the best spirits and cheerfully made every exertion to provide for the enjoyment of the pleasure-seekers as soon as the more substantial objects of the Fair—the business part—had ended. The quantity of stock on the field was not large, and was thinner than for some years past, but prices ranged high and a good sale was the result. The pleasure portion of the community were, however, sadly disappointed because later in the day the wind rose and the rain fell and a storm arose which became so violent that one or two of the standings were thrown down, and the shows were obliged to haul down their pictures and close. Notwithstanding the rain, however, great numbers of people had poured into the town and as there was no possibility of their visiting the field to enjoy themselves, they therefore went to the several hostelries, attracted by the sound of violins, and passed the day on 'the light fantastic toe'. As a day of business for tradesmen of the town it was a complete disaster, it was remembered as a Fair during which the tradesmen had never done so little. It was confidently asserted that the Fair had proved a failure to all who sought to make money by amusement, and to all also who sought amusement as a recreation.

The Pig Cross Revels took place in June. It was stated that this Revel had not shared the fate which time bestows on most things mortal, but on the contrary seemed to have revived with redoubled vigour this year, and the old English sports were even more popular. Donkey racing, jumping in sacks, grinning through horse collars, and foot racing by ladies and gentlemen. The attendance was described as numerous if not fashionable.

In February a fine new ship, the *Pathfinder,* the property of Bridgwater merchants, was built in Bridgwater by Messrs Axford & Sons, Bridgwater people were very proud of this vessel which was lying in the floating dock being prepared to convey passengers and goods direct from Bridgwater to New York. It marked a new era in local history and was confidently felt to herald a new and better state of affairs for the port. The ship left Bridgwater on Sunday, 8 March at about seven a.m. for New York. She had on board a full complement of emigrants, about one hundred and thirty in number. Upwards of 5,000 people lined the banks of the river to witness her departure, and when she was towed by the steamer out of the outer basin, she was saluted with cannon and the hearty 'hurrahs' of the spectators. For some weeks the *Pathfinder* had been a great attraction in Bridgwater and she had been visited by thousands, and her superior fittings elicited the marked and decided approval of all who had seen her. On leaving the basis she proceeded to sea with the same tide, which, for a vessel of her size, and drawing as she did 15ft. of water, was a feat not often accomplished from the port. The *Pathfinder* reached the Channel at nine a.m.; the steamer continued with her as far as Minehead, which she reached at 12 noon. Messrs Axford & Sons were congratulated for their spirit and received great credit for the undertaking. It was the most spirited enterprise which had ever been undertaken on behalf of the port, and they had the earnest good wishes of their townsmen for the success of the venture and the safety of the vessel. The emigrants left in good spirit and received the generous farewell, not only of their friends, but of the thousands of spectators who witnessed her departure. The *Pathfinder* was described as a fine, new, first-class, fast-sailing, clipper-built barque of 800 tons burden. The commander was William Loveless, and the voyage took 30 days.

The Mayor was Mr Thomas Ford.

1853 On 26 March a serious accident occurred in Friarn Street, Bridgwater, when some people riding 'Dandy Horses' through the streets at about six o'clock in the evening at a rate of 10 miles an hour, ran over a little child, about four years of age and broke its right arm and seriously injured its thigh. Mr H. Symes immediately attended the child, rendering every aid in his power. The father of the child was a brickmaker.

In January a curious circumstance occurred. The late Mr Henry Hurford of Pound Farm, Haygrove, Bridgwater, left by his will a favourite horse to his nephew, Mr George Cook. The bequest was subject to the condition that his nephew should not part with the horse and that when it had done its last job it should be killed and buried. The horse was engaged to draw a gravestone from Mr Samuel Hurford's premises in North Street, which was to cover his late master's resting place in Durleigh Churchyard. The horse did carry the stone to Durleigh and returned with the truck which was deposited in Squibbs' yard in North Street. The horse was then led across the street to Samuel Hurford's, where, having performed its last service to its deceased master, it dropped down dead. Mr Cook buried the horse according to his uncle's wishes.

In December a fine Austrian vessel of 400 tons coming up the river on a Saturday morning, ran aground off Dunball and received so much damage that water was running through and over her. The cargo consisted of wheat for Messrs Spiller and Browne and would realise little of its original value. It was fortunately insured.

Three vessels with emigrants left Bridgwater.

John Clark of Bridgwater, inventor of waterproof clothing, died.

In December magistrates of the Borough refused to grant Mr Palmer a licence for a theatre. It was stated 'Why should the inhabitants of Bridgwater indulge in theatrical entertainments to the danger and risk of contaminating their morals? They have not the strength to guard against this sad danger'.

On 17 March people were startled by the sound of a band of music with varied cheering and groaning. On enquiry it was found that many journeymen shoemakers were parading the town in marching order, calling on every master shoemaker to demand an advance in their wages. Those who acquiesced in the terms proposed were greeted with three cheers, whilst groans were delivered for each obdurate master. The men were all respectably dressed, and there was no conception, until the procession was actually seen, that so many shoemakers earned their living in Bridgwater.

In December the members of the Saltlands Bowling Society celebrated their 12th anniversary at the *Lamb* inn. More than 30 members and their friends assembled on the occasion. The dinner was served at four o'clock and reflected great credit on the landlord and his wife. The viands consisted of every delicacy, and were served in capital style. The wines were also of first-rate quality. During the evening some excellent glees, duets and songs were sung, with Mr Andrews presiding at the pianoforte. Several of these songs were from the clever pen of the local townsman, Mr Burrington. The evening was spent in perfect harmony, and the company retired at a late hour delighted with their evening's entertainment.

On Friday, 8 January, the Annual Tradesmen's Dinner was held at the *Royal Clarence* hotel. It was numerously attended; Robert Ford Esq. presided, and the vice-chair was occupied by Mr James Leaker. The dinner, as always at the *Clarence,* was excellently served, and wines were of the richest quality. After the withdrawal of the cloth the usual loyal and patriotic toasts were proposed and enthusiastically responded to. The evening was spent with the greatest conviviality and its enjoyment was enhanced by the singing of Mr Babbage,

Mr George Knight, Mr Peter Horsey, Mr W. Green, and other gentlemen. The company did not break up until a late hour.

The Mayor was Mr George Parker.

1854 On a Sunday evening in March a crowded congregation attended St Mary's Parish Church; but before half the service was over the gas lights began flickering and ultimately nearly all went out. The villainous smell of escaping gas and the want of light compelled the congregation to beat an immediate and hasty retreat. It was not discovered on whose shoulders the blame fell, but there was gross inattention somewhere.

On 28 July the annual Navigation Survey of the River Parrett by the Bridgwater Corporation took place in a steamer called the *Rapid* which was fitted up and gaily decorated for the occasion. The steamer left the quay at 8.30 a.m. and proceeded down the river accompanied by a band of music to the Holme. A large company attended, and as the Mayor was unable to attend through ill-health, Alderman Ford was called upon to act as Commander. The Worthy Commander informed the company that there would be sufficient time to allow of their proceeding to Porlock Bay and landing there—with the view to lightening the vessel of the immense amount of cargo and provisions with which she was stored, hampers of which were piled on deck in an alarming manner. There were no less than 2,000 people to witness the return of the steamer; it was described as one of the most pleasant trips for some years past.

On the evening of 9 November, notwithstanding the notice of the Mayor, Guy Fawkes Night was had with more than wonted spirit. A glorious bonfire was made on the Cornhill and fireworks were very plentiful. A large procession headed by a band and accompanied by numerous banners paraded the town carrying a capital 'Guy' with a light borne before him and a splendid full-size model of the Emperor Nicholas, got up 'regardless of expense' in traditional costume. After parading the town for about two hours, both the rascals were pitched into the bonfire amidst the cheers of more than 1,000 spectators. The evening passed off without accident, save the inevitable singeing of coats and whiskers. Some of the disguises of the squibbers were exceedingly amusing.

On the 23 and 24 August the Bridgwater and West Somerset Races revived their Annual Meetings and the organisers were determined to render the two days sport credit and honour to the town and county. It was many years since Bridgwater was identified with racing, which had dropped off in the county due to jockeyship and the bartering and arranging of races which too frequently had prevailed to the extinction of good sportsmanship, and to the disgust of the company and the supporters of gentlemanly amusement. However, when these ungentlemanly practices were eradicated, all were eager to encourage the sport. The Races were described as unusually good, held in gloriously fine weather and the attendance in the field was excellent.

In November, what was described as 'Oyster-Shell Nuisance', the throwing of oyster shells in the streets of the town, was an increasing and dangerous practice. There had been several narrow escapes from accidents, when horses slipped over the shells. It was hoped that the nuisance would be stopped.

The Mayor was Mr William Browne.

1855 On 16 June the Council's main concern was the refusal of the then Vicar of Bridgwater to preach a sermon at St Mary's Church on Sunday afternoons. In the Minute Book of the Town Council the following resolution was passed: 'That in the opinion of the Council the refusal or neglect of the Rev. R. C. James to preach, or cause to be preached, a sermon in St Mary's Church in the afternoon of each Sunday during the year will be an evasion of his appointment as afternoon lecturer and that a copy of this resolution be sent to the Bishop'. The vexed question was the subject of a special meeting in July, at which the Town Clerk, Mr J. H. Carslake, was instructed professionally to wait on his Lordship the Bishop for the purpose of presenting a memorial. It appears that the Vicar won the day as the following letter from the Bishop was before the Council at a special meeting in August:

'I have no power whatever to force on your Vicar, the Rev T. G. James, the performance of an afternoon service so long as a second service was given by him, the Deed of Donation not specifying the time at which the service shall be given.'

The number of vessels using the port of Bridgwater in this year was 2,314 of a total tonnage of 112,395, and the duties paid were £584 0s. 3d.

During February the cold weather was excessively severe; the river, a few yards below the bridge, was completely blocked up with ice and navigation was suspended. The seamen of the port were completely 'frozen out' of employment by the severe weather, and they went around the town soliciting contributions from the various householders to enable them to keep their bodies and souls together, which the extreme cold and absence of food was likely to affect. The severity of the weather affected the health of many people in the town and neighbourhood. At nearly every house influenza, or as it was popularly termed 'the flu', had seized some of the inmates and dealt with them most roughly. The season had been more than usually fatal to persons of advanced age, and the registrar's return of deaths was far above the average.

An unhealthy symptom in March of this year. Some grumblers complained of the dullness of trade, amongst these, however, were three exceptions: doctors, undertakers and parsons, who had plenty of business. It could not be said that it 'looked healthy'.

On 27 February a skating match was held at Westonzoyland between two gentlemen of the town, Messrs Symons and Reeves. The distance skated over was one mile, and Mr Reeves was the winner by about one hundred yards, even though Mr Symons had taken the lead for the first half mile.

The snow and sleet storm which visited the town on a Friday night in February was the severest that had been experienced for years. It came upon roofs already laden with snow and caused many an unpleasant night adventure. As the gutters were already full the water penetrated where it could through roofs and ceilings and nearly half the town suffered more or less from the infliction. It was described as 'thus realising to some very little extent the horrors of a night in the Crimea'. Many had to shift bed and quarters from the insinuating enemy. Some persons, it was stated, had to sit in bed with umbrellas in order to throw off the bold intruder and many were compelled to cut and run to save themselves from a ducking. Severe losses were sustained by several people in the town. Mr James Leaker of the *Golden Ball* hotel had 2,000 bushels of malt ruined.

The manufacture of plaster of Paris was started, which added trade to the town, by Messrs Barham Bros who had erected steam mills for the purpose.

The Bridgwater Mercury was established, in response to a memorial signed by the principal inhabitants of the town, by Mr William A. Woodley, proprietor of *The Somerset County Gazette* at Taunton. He appointed Mr George Thomas Donisthorpe as editor, and the paper was printed and published in King Street. Its first issue was dated 18 June 1855. It was in that year that the stamp duty on newspapers was repealed. It was then a four-page paper, price 3d. It opened under favourable auspices, with a subscribers' roll containing over 300 local names. It was printed and published in Ball's Lane (now King Street), by Mr James Brown Morgan. *The Mercury* immediately became the most popular local paper, and even in its earliest days it showed great capacity for local news, which soon carried it far in advance of its two rivals. The trivial occurrences that make up the social life of a country town were faithfully chronicled and the more important events were given at length that was quite unique in local journalism. It was well supported by advertisers; in the year following its introduction it was enlarged to eight pages. Success still attended it, and another enlargement later took place. Its circulation had meanwhile extended far beyond the town, and the name was altered to *The Bridgwater Mercury and Western Counties Herald.* In 1866 the editorship was entrusted to Mr J. T. Dunsford and under his able guidance the journal built up the high reputation it now enjoys. The Bridgwater public on one memorable occasion showed their appreciation of his worth by making him a handsome presentation. In 1884 Mr Dunsford was admitted to partnership.

The Mayor was Mr John Browne.

1856 A free Reading Room was established in Taunton road.

The number of vessels using the port of Bridgwater in this year was 2,281 of a total tonnage of 110,994, and the duties paid totalled £576 10s. 6d.

Originally an 'Island' of narrow buildings ran up the middle of the High Street all the way from the Cornhill to the Mansion House (No. 32). As new buildings went up, the building line was moved forward by several feet (i.e. from No. 8 the *Clarence* as far as No. 18 the Trustee Savings Bank).

The remainder of 'the Island' continued to stand for many years. The buildings along the north side had always been butchers' shops. For this reason 'the north part of the High Street' was often called 'the Shambles'. The end of the Island came in January 1856 when the last three buildings were demolished.

As old houses on the northern edge were replaced by new ones, they were kept back to the original building line. For this reason there is a very wide pavement outside Nos. 20 and 32. No 20 is still the Mansion House, but No. 26 (the *Bull and Butcher*) has ceased to function as a public house as has No. 20 (the *Old Oak*).

The buildings between and including No. 10 and No. 26 are due to be replaced by something quite different, in order to open up the Clare Street area behind them. This scheme is called the Central Area Development Scheme.

On Monday, 21 July, great interest was occasioned when the leviathan steamer *Talasien* arrived at Bridgwater from Cardiff, bringing more than 200 excursionists. Her length was 130ft., her engines 80 horsepower, and she possessed accommodation for 600 people.

The Mayor was Mr W. D. Bath.

1857 A Russian cannon, which was captured in the Crimean War, was presented to the town. It was met with bands of music and drawn through the town in procession. The cannon was later placed on a pedestal enclosed by an iron railing, on a spot between the river and the road in Salmon Parade. In 1886 it was decided to move it to a piece of land at the junction of the Bristol and Bath roads and the site became known as 'The Cannon'.

The Crimean cannon itself was removed during the Second World War as salvaged metal.

On 10 June there appeared a new paper in Bridgwater called *The Somersetshireman and Leader,* published weekly at two pence. It lasted for 13 weeks.

Wednesday, 7 October was kept as a 'day of humiliation' by royal proclamation, with reference to the Indian Mutiny. Business was entirely suspended and special services were held in every Church and Chapel in Bridgwater. The attendance was very large. A fund for relieving the sufferers in the Mutiny was afterwards started and £150 was collected in the town and neighbourhood and forwarded to the Mayor of London.

The launching of a fine ship took place from the Crowpill Shipbuilding Yard on Saturday, 24 April at 7.30 a.m. in the presence of about three hundred persons. She was the sailing vessel *Admiral Blake* of 190 tons, length 100ft., breadth 21st., and depth 12ft 6ins. Three flags were temporarily hoisted during the launch: the Union Jack; the Borough Arms; and a third contained the words 'Admiral Blake'. She was laid down in August 1856 and was a credit to her builder, Mr John Gough. The vessel was named after the celebrated naval hero.

At the General Election held on 28 March the result was as follows:

Colonel Charles K. Kemys-Tynte (Liberal)	330
Mr Alexander William Kinglake (Liberal)	301
Mr Brent Spencer Follett (Conservative)	203

Colonel Tynte and Mr Kinglake were elected.

On 5 January, Bridgwater had the honour of being the first town in the county to denounce the 'Income Tax'. A public meeting at the Town Hall convened by its chief magistrate was most influentially attended. There was a large attendance of all classes of the town and all those with differing political beliefs were drawn together on this occasion. Bridgwater, in the presence of its two representatives, pronounced most unmistakably against the 'Income Tax' altogether. The ratepayers and burgesses resolved to adopt every constitutional means to obtain its immediate and total repeal. They declared the tax to be unequal and unjust in principle, to be inquisitorial and offensive in its assessment, and derogatory to the freedom of Englishmen, and demanded its total repeal from and after 5 April next.

The number of vessels using the port of Bridgwater was 2,444 of a total tonnage of 115,551 and the duties paid were £603 13s. 3d.

On 30 December the street called Ball's Lane was renamed King Street.

The Mayor was Mr J. Ruddock.

1858 It was stated on 30 June that few of the townspeople were aware that a ferry across the river, with landing steps on either side down to low water mark, was available; but such was the case. The ferry was made just on the south side of the Docks and opposite the cement works which had recently been erected by Mr Barham. On payment of ½d. any person could be ferried over. By this accommodation a saving of nearly 1,100 yards was made by those who required to go from one side of the river to the other. It was hoped that the undertaking would be supported.

It was noticed in October that great efforts had been made by the enterprising tradesmen of the town in the improvement of their premises and the extension of their businesses. The handsome building and extensive showrooms erected by Messrs Nicholls, linen drapers on the Cornhill, started a move in the right direction. This example was followed by Mr Whitby, stationer; and later by Messrs Phillips & Son, who submitted a more imposing appearance in front of their premises affording them vastly increased business. Messrs Thomas Bros, ironmongers, had just completed a most handsome building. Mr Holmes, the linen draper, was still busily engaged in putting in some very large and beautiful plate glass windows. Mr West, stationer, altered his entire front, and Messrs Young & Symonds had just completed a like improvement.

On 10 February a movement was started to stop hairdressing and shaving on Sundays in the town. A notice was issued by eight of the hairdressers of the town intimating that after that month they would not open their shops for the transaction of business on Sundays. Steps would be taken to compel those who refused to sign to do so in accordance with the resolution of the majority.

On the evening of 11 October one of the most destructive fires for many years occurred at the extensive timber yards of Messrs Axford & Co., East Quay. A considerable quantity of prepared timber was lying in the yard at that time, as well as massive lengths of valuable mahogany, nearly the whole of which was destroyed. The entire framework of the saw mills fell prey to the devastating flames; also the machinery and a 12 h.p. engine were much damaged. The stock and premises were insured.

The Mayor was Mr J. Ruddock.

1859 At the General Election held on 30 April Colonel Charles K. Kemys-Tynte (Liberal) and Mr A. W. Kinglake (Liberal) were elected. The result was as follows:

Colonel Charles K. Kemys-Tynte (Liberal)	290
Mr A. W. Kinglake (Liberal)	279
Mr Henry Padwick (Conservative)	230
Mr Henry Westrop (Conservative)	208

In January the Y.M.C.A. was established on the Cornhill.

On Monday, 27 June, a rare fish was caught in the River Parrett just above Dunball. It proved to be a large sturgeon weighing 1½ cwt. It was conveyed to Bridgwater Market where it excited much curiosity, and was afterwards sold at 5d. and 6d. a pound.

The Agapemone—the 'Abode of Love'—a strange community of religious visionaries, was founded at Spaxton by Brother Prince. Brother Prince began as a Doctor of Medicine and later took orders in the Anglican Church. His community, which did not lack funds, at one time numbered 200 people, of whom five were parsons. The 'Abode of Love' was surrounded by walls 15ft. high enclosing a delicious domain of about five acres. Although they hid themselves for the most part behind the high walls of their 'Abode of Love', they managed to make their presence as imposing as possible. There was quite a commotion in the town when Brother Prince drove into it in great splendour with four bay horses, outriders, postillions, and—to give a touch of the formidable —a number of bloodhounds. Sometimes he would stop on the Cornhill where the Blake statue now stands, and there much speaking and exhortation took place. The approach was announced by heralds crying out loudly at intervals 'Blessed is he that cometh in the name of the Lord'. There was in the minds of certain people, no doubt, some awe at this strange scene. To the majority it was merely a pretty sight; to some it was only a ridiculous one. The tradesmen of the town were required to address their parcels to 'My Lord the Prince', and a story still runs that the chief drapers lost their custom by refusing to comply with the condition. The double insolence of appropriating the title 'Lord', and transmitting 'Mr Prince' into 'Prince' suggests a touch of morbid megalomania. Brother Prince claimed in some sort of way to be the Messiah.

The Mayor was Mr R. Woodland.

1860 The telephone was first tried out in Eastover.

The Free Libraries Act was adopted by the town, and the following year saw the opening of a municipal reading room in Friarn Street.

The Bridgwater School of Art, in George Street, was opened in January.

The Wesleyan Chapel in King Street was restored and enlarged. It was originally built in 1816.

In November, Colonel Charles K. Kemys-Tynte, better known as 'The Old Colonel' died at the age of eighty-two. He had for many years been one of the best-known and most generous benefactors to the town and had faithfully represented the borough in six successive parliaments.

The Mayor was Mr Robert Ford.

1861 On 2 January arrangements had been completed for the removal of the Post Office, the business of which had hitherto been carried on in St Mary Street, to premises on the Eastern Quay. It was stated that the new arrangement would prove of special benefit, the office in St Mary Street having been found so extremely warm and inconvenient as to cause the employees considerable hindrance, and much personal discomfort, in carrying out their duties.

The population of the town was 12,120.

A newspaper called *The Bridgwater Standard, Burnham Times and West of England Gazette* was established on Wednesday, 16 October by Conrad Stokes. It was printed and published in Court Street. It ceased with the issue of 26 March 1870.

Turkish Baths situated in York Buildings were opened. They were well fitted up. The proprietor was Mr John Hurman.

In May, what was described as 'Teetotal Intemperance' was much in the news. It was thought that the local authorities in Bridgwater had not done wisely in permitting the open-air addresses of a teetotal delegate in the streets of the town. For several evenings a man named James Teare had collected a crowd on the Quay in front of two public houses and had held forth not so much in praise of teetotal abstinence, but in virulent abuse of brewers,publicans and all who deal in intoxicating liquors, and so personal were his remarks to the proprietors and frequenters of public houses that angry feelings were aroused, and there were dangers that the peace of the town would be disturbed. It was stated that teetotalism should be advocated with judgement; peacably, quietly, with good temper, and charity. Many good and sincere men who had taken up the cause of teetotalism believing it to be a powerful means of good to people thought it was a matter of regret that the cause should be injured by intemperate advocacy.

The Mayor was Mr John Browne.

1862 The *Martin,* a schooner of 115 tons, the Captain of which was William Johnson, and belonging to Messrs Colthurst, Symons & Co., left Newcastle for Bridgwater with a cargo of coal. During the rough weather in the English Channel, the vessel took her course towards the coast of France, where she went ashore. The vessel lay for some time until she eventually fell over and went to pieces becoming a complete wreck. The crew were fortunately landed safely.

Henry Westropp Esq., later M.P. for Bridgwater, presented to the borough a portrait of Admiral Robert Blake. It represents a young man with moustache and beard, dressed in black velvet, over which falls a broad white collar, edged with lace. The portrait is generally regarded as an authentic one, and the town was congratulated on such a possession.

The foundation stone of the Congregational Church in Fore Street was laid on 25 August by Mr Samuel Morley.

The Bridgwater Teetotal Club was formed. Once established the Club made rapid progress and at one time had a muster-roll of over 400 persons.

Alterations and additions were made to the Infirmary in this year and soon afterwards another house adjoining was purchased for £205. Additions were again made in 1876 and 1895.

The Mayor was Mr John Browne.

1863 It was stated in April that the following address was in course of signature by the townspeople of Bridgwater—'Sir, we, the undersigned, understand that a bill demanding that public houses be closed from Saturday nights until Monday mornings has been presented to the Commons. We believe that such a measure is at variance with the boasted impartiality of the English law'.

In accordance with the resolution of the Town Council, a large amount of the Bridgwater Corporation property was sold by auction to raise money for the proposed Town Hall, the amount realised being £2,891. Work on the new building would begin immediately.

A public meeting was held on 12 February at three o'clock in the afternoon to consider the subject of erecting a new Town Hall.

The Mayor was Mr John Ruddock.

1864 Messrs Hennett, Spink & Else of the Bridgwater Iron Foundry accepted the contract for erecting the new bridge over the Thames at Hampton Court.

A beautiful barque was launched from the yard of Mr John Gough at Bridgwater. As the vessel glided off the ways she was named *Cesarea.* She was of 400 tons and the largest vessel to be launched for many years.

On Friday the Mayor, Aldermen and Burgesses of Bridgwater sent congratulations to Her Majesty the Queen and the Prince and Princess of Wales on the happy and auspicious event of a birth of a son to the royal couple.

A strike took place amongst a number of Bridgwater brickmakers. About ninety of them left their work because the piece or task work that they were given was to be increased. A public meeting was held, at which 3,000 attended. There seemed to be great sympathy for the strikers among the general public, and fellow workmen subscribed towards the strike, which did not look like ending.

The United Kingdom Telegraph Co. opened offices on the West Quay, and messages could be sent to any of their stations at a uniform rate of 1s. for 20 words. A telegraph office had long been wanted in the town.

On 22 September the opening ceremony of the Fore Street Congregational Church took place. It was followed by a dinner at the Market House attended by about 600 people, and a tea at the Sion Chapel at which 1,100 were present.

The Mayor was Mr John Browne.

1865 Mr John Browne, a notable brick and tile manufacturer, was in his fifth year of office as Mayor of Bridgwater, and was presented by the inhabitants with a fine full-length portrait of himself, which he in turn gave to the Corporation for the Town Hall, together with paintings of Queen Victoria and the Prince Consort. All three pictures were painted by a Bridgwater artist, Mr. W. Baker.

At the General Election held on 12 July the result was as follows:

Mr Henry Westropp (Conservative)	328
Mr Alexander William Kinglake (Liberal)	257
Sir John Villers Shelley (Liberal)	237

Mr H. Westropp and Mr A. W. Kinglake were elected. Mr H. Westropp was unseated later and another election followed in June 1866.

The Bridgwater Town Council considered a communication from the Bristol and Exeter Railway Company, expressing their intention to extend their railway system across the River Parrett to the Docks and to Bridgwater Cattle Market. The Council did not like the idea of a railway bridge, which it was feared might interfere with the navigation of the river. The Council appointed a committee to consider the scheme.

The Town Hall and Municipal Buildings in High Street was opened on 6 July.

1866 In November, in consequence of the report of medical officers on the sanitary conditions of the town, the Mayor called a public meeting of the inhabitants to consider the question of a new water supply, in response to which a large and influential gathering of townspeople was held when there was a unanimous expression of opinion in favour of a new water supply.

James Hartnell of Bridgwater died on 26 February aged 102 years and six months old. A memorial stone to him is inserted in the wall by the south entrance of St Mary's Church.

An outbreak of cholera occurred in Bridgwater and impure water taken from wells in the eastern end of the town was believed to have been the cause of the outbreak. In that area there were a number of potato fields and the haulms were allowed to rot on the surface, which was also used by cattle. Rain washed the poisons from decomposed vegetables and animal matter into the wells, with the result that cholera claimed a number of victims.

A Parliamentary By-Election was held on 7 June and the result was as follows:

Mr George Patton (Conservative)	301
Mr Walter Bagehot (Liberal)	294

Mr Patton was elected with a majority of seven.

A Parliamentary By-Election was held on 12 July and the result was as follows:

Mr Philip Vanderbyl (Liberal)	312
Mr George Patton (Conservative)	276

Mr Philip Vanderbyl was elected with a majority of thirty-six.

At a public meeting held on 10 February it was unanimously agreed that the purchase of the Bridgwater and Taunton Canal and the Docks by the Bristol and Exeter Railway Company, and the extension of their railway to the Docks by means of a drawbridge, and the laying down by them of the narrow gauge line as proposed by their Bill now before Parliament, would be of great benefit to the town and would materially facilitate and increase the traffic in minerals and goods which then existed. Also it was thought to be for the advantage of the town that the Bill pending in Parliament for making a narrow gauge railway from Bridgwater through the villages of Bawdrip, Cossington, Chilton Polden, Edington, Catcott, and Shapwick to join the Somerset and Dorset line at the last-named place, be passed into a law. This scheme failed.

The Mayor was Mr George Parker.

1867 The number of Electors rose from 700 to 1,500.

Sunday, 8 March, is remarkable on account of the fire which destroyed Wembdon Church.

The black-faced clock on the tower of St Mary's Church was removed and a new clock erected; also another bell, the eighth and largest, was added. They were erected by voluntary contributions.

Tea was 2s. 6d. to 4s. per lb.; gin 2s. per bottle; brandy 2s. 2d.; whisky from 2s. 1d.; and rum 2s. per bottle.

The Teetotal Club anniversary was celebrated on Whit Monday in a field at the top of West Street. The members marched through the town in procession carrying flags and headed by the Nether Stowey Band.

A public meeting was held on 27 September in the Town Hall called by the Mayor, Mr John B. Hammill, to consider the question of an increased water supply for the borough.

1868 Messrs Knight's Wine and Spirit Vaults in the High Street, the *King's Head,* advertised India Pale Ale at 4s. 6d. per dozen pints, and claret at 18s. per dozen bottles. Family Ale was advertised at 10d. and 1s. per gallon, India Pale at 4s. 6d. per dozen pints, and claret at 18s. per dozen bottles. Family Ale was advertised at 10s. and 1s. per gallon, India Pale Ale at 40s. a barrel. Tea was 2s. a lb. from Mr F. J. Saunders, the proprietor of the Western Tea Mart in St Mary Street. There was a cut-price firm in London advertising in *The Bridgwater Mercury,* offering 'strong to fine black tea at 1s. 6d. a lb'. A Chinese Caddy of 16lb. of tea was offered at 40s.

At the General Election held on 17 November the result was as follows:

Mr Alexander William Kinglake (Liberal)	731
Sir Philip Vanderbyl (Liberal)	725
Mr Henty Westropp (Conservative)	681
Mr Charles William Gray (Conservative)	650

Mr A. W. Kinglake and Sir P. Vanderbyl were elected, but both were later unseated.

Extensive warehouses were erected at the Docks and the West and East Quays.

The 27 July was a proud day for the Bridgwater Volunteers, and indeed for all the inhabitants, as it witnessed the arrival of that much-coveted prize the Wimbledon Trophy, in the town. Lieutenant J. B. Carslake, of the 5th Somerset (Bridgwater) Volunteers was declared the winner. The occasion was celebrated with great rejoicing, the Church bells were rung and cannon fired on the river bank. Lieutenant Carslake was accorded a great public reception, the streets and houses were beautifully decorated and beflagged. All business in the town was suspended, and the inhabitants turned out in full force to honour their young townsman.

The Mayor was Mr Joseph R. Smith.

1869 One of the highlights of 1869 was the enquiry held which resulted in the disenfranchisement of the Borough of Bridgwater following enquiries held in London in which three M.P.s were unseated. The first was Mr Henry Westropp, Conservative, who was elected on 12 July 1865. At that election there were three candidates for two seats and the result was as follows:

Mr Henry Westropp (Conservative)	328
Mr Alexander William Kingslake (Liberal)	257
Sir William Shelley (Liberal)	237

A petition was organised on behalf of the two Liberal candidates and was heard before a select committee of the House of Commons, which found that extensive bribery and other practices had prevailed both before and during the election, and Mr Henry Westropp was unseated. Out of the electorate of 598 the committee found that 25 people were guilty of bribery and corrupt practices, and that 173 were bribed.

Two further M.P.s were unseated: Mr Philip Vanderbyl (Liberal); and Mr A. W. Kinglake (Liberal). This occurred after the election of 17 November 1868, at which there were four candidates for two seats. The result was as follows:

Mr A. W. Kinglake (Liberal)	731
Mr P. Vanderbyl (Liberal)	725
Mr H. Westropp (Conservative)	681
Mr H. Gray (Conservative)	650

A petition was presented by the Conservatives and was heard before Mr Justice Blackburn at the Town Hall, Bridgwater, in Frebuary 1869, and it was found that Mr Kinglake and Mr Vanderbyl were guilty of bribery and corruption and were unseated. As a result of the report of Mr Justice Blackburn to the committee, an enquiry into the existence of bribery and corruption at the election of 1868 and previous elections was ordered. This commission sat at the Town Hall, Bridgwater, from Monday, 23 August until Saturday 16 October 1868, during which 46,500 questions were asked and answered, and 515 people were examined, many on several occasions.

It was as a result of this enquiry that the Borough was disenfranchised.

The proceedings of the Bribery Committee were dull. Sharp questions were shot at the man in the witness stand by members of the commission. Any answers revealing the guilt of other men would be jotted down and then in their turn these men would be called up, and be put through the same searching procedure. It must have been a nerve-racking time for all implicated. In the old election days when the borough had two representatives in Parliament political feeling ran very high and the town was naturally very lively before and during the election. The exciting feeling that yet another golden election was imminent kept lots of people moving to see what could be done about it. Coloured ribbons and rosettes showed party loyalties. The candidates and their fashionably-dressed wives dashed about the town in well-appointed pair-horsed landaus, with horses and drivers dressed up in buff or blue party colours, helping to keep things moving. Apparently they spent the time canvassing the electors. Old electioneering methods differed greatly from modern ones, campaigns were shorter, though much more money was spent, which must have caused many a defeated candidate to rue the day he first heard of Bridgwater!

The practice of giving and receiving bribes was engaged in with much openness. A mysterious stranger was introduced into the town, known as 'The Man in the Moon' who located himself at one of the public houses of the party and 'received visitors' in a darkened room. In exchange for cards bearing a private mark, he, in solemn silence, distributed 'cartridges' or 'samples of tea', i.e., rolls of money, among those voters who had 'qualified' for possession of the card mentioned. Sometimes it happened that the payment for votes commenced a fortnight before the polling day, and it was no matter for surprise that in numerous instances bribes were received by voters of both parties.

At the election of 1859 about five hundred of these 'balanced men' who had received £10 each for their votes from the Conservatives previous to the polling, were seized upon by the Liberals on the morning of the election given £10 each, marched up to the hustings, and their votes recorded for the Liberal candidates.

Various tales went about as to where the 'Man in the Moon' operated from: one was a darkened room in a small public house; another, that he was concealed in a very large barrel and passed out the money through the bung hole. His comings and goings were all very secret and were apparently unobserved, and no one ever discovered his real identity or where he came from. The Bribery Commission and Report, however, saw these matters differently, and Bridgwater lost its representation in Parliament as a separate borough until 1885 when it was restored as a new Division of the County.

The Bridgwater Oil and Cake Mills at the Docks were opened. At first about fifteen workmen were employed, but eventually up to 70 men worked here.

On Tuesday, 3 August, a Brigade Review of Somersetshire Volunteers was held near Bridgwater. There was a banquet at the Town Hall for the officers who were entertained by the Earl of Cork. The town was decorated for the event which caused great excitement and occasioned a general holiday.

The Bridgwater Summer Fair was held on Wednesday, 7 July. In former years it was numerously attended by dealers and plentifully supplied with horses of the best quality. For some time past, however, it had been gradually on the decline and on this occasion the falling off was especially noticeable. The Fair was held in Eastover in the vicinity of the *Commercial* hotel, where the horses were exhibited. Carriage horses were 'few and far between'. Hacks, likewise few in number, ranged from £12 to £20. Some good working cart-horses realised as much as £45, the remainder averaging from £20 to £35. Ponies, not broken in, were disposed of at £6 to £10.

The Mayor was Mr George Bryant Sully.

1870 On the night of 7 February a destructive fire occurred on the south side of Cornhill.

Wembdon Church was re-opened after the disastrous fire which occurred on Sunday, 8 March 1867; the Church having been restored and rebuilt.

A newspaper called *The Bridgwater Argus* was established.

The number of vessels entering the port of Bridgwater was 3,772 of a total tonnage of 208,629.

The new Post Office in High Street was opened on 1 October.

On 1 January the Election Commissioners recommended the disenfranchisement of Bridgwater. The verdict was 'We find that corrupt practices have extensively prevailed at the last election, and at every preceding election for the Borough of Bridgwater into which we have enquired up to and inclusive of the earliest in date, that is to say the General Election of the 30th of April to the 3rd of May 1831'.

A public meeting was held in July to call attention to the necessity for the immediate removal of the existing bridge crossing the River Parrett, and the substitution of a new bridge. The new bridge had to be constructed to deal with the increasing traffic of the town, and at the same time to put a stop to the serious accidents which were almost of daily occurrence on the bridge owing to its steep declivity on either side.

On 30 December the Mayor convened a public meeting to be held in the Grand Jury Room to take into consideration the propriety of re-opening the soup kitchens for the relief of the distress caused to the poor by the inclement state of the weather.

1871 A newspaper called *The Bridgwater Gazette, Somerset and Devon Chronicle and West of England Advertiser* was established.

The Telescopic Bridge over the River Parrett connecting the railway from Bridgwater Goods Station to the Docks and the Northgate Brewery was completed in March. The bridge was opened by steam engine and was preceded by the blowing of a whistle. The bridge was frequently opened when vessels had to come up right along the West and East Quays to load and unload.

The number of vessels entering the port of Bridgwater was 3,595 of a total of 196,538 tons.

A new organ was placed in the North Chapel of St Mary's Church at a cost of nearly £1,000.

The population of the town was 12,636.

Property was sold by the Bridgwater Corporation to the Bristol and Exeter Railway Company.

The Mayor was Mr H. F. Nicholls.

1872 The number of vessels entering the port of Bridgwater was 3,829 of a total of 201,875 tons.

In January, the Mayor, Mr H. F. Nicholls, convened a public meeting to take into consideration the propriety of reorganising the system of coal relief and other matters connected with the general relief of the poor.

The Municipal Borough's Infectious Diseases Hospital was erected at a cost of £400 and could hold eight patients.

1873 The number of vessels entering the port of Bridgwater was 3,979 of a total tonnage of 212,197.

The Mayor was Mr Joseph R. Smith.

1874 In this year the 'Bridgwater Training Home for Girls' was founded. It proved itself an admirable institution and it was instrumental in helping young girls to a good start in life and showing them how to earn a living in domestic service.

The Mayor was Mr Joseph R. Smith.

1875 The *Three Tuns* inn at Penel Orlieu was purchased by the Bridgwater Corporation for part of the site of the new Cattle Market. The site is now occupied by the *Classic* theatre.

The citizens of the town had a great thrill when they witnessed a 10-foot 'Bore' sweep up the river, believed to be the highest ever.

The old Bridgwater Gaol in Fore Street was closed and moved to the Police Station in High Street.

Fire destroyed the *Globe* hotel, Eastover on 31 May.

A new Corn Exchange in the Market House Building on the Cornhill was opened on 19 May. An open courtyard in the middle of the building was roofed in with glass, which is as we see it today.

The Mayor was Mr George Wilton.

1876 Holy Trinity Church, Taunton Road, was restored and re-seated.

A 43-page booklet entitled *The Ancient History of Bridgwater,* was published by George Parker of Bridgwater. It did not enjoy much success. Some of the work was in verse. George Parker was quite an accomplished writer and had a fairly sound knowledge of local history. He had probably delved into the archives and quoted from documents then stored in the town gaol.

The Bible Christian Chapel in Polden Street was built with a seating capacity for 250 persons.

The Mayor was Mr George Wilton.

1877 The Somerset Drainage Commission was established.

The Cattle Market situated at Penel Orlieu on the site of the present *Classic* theatre was opened.

The Mayor was Mr James Leaker.

1878 The tender of Messrs Chedzoy & Sons in the sum of £3,234 9s. 3d. was accepted for the erection of Albert Street School.

St John's Cemetery in the Bristol Road was opened in August. It is about thirteen acres in extent and contains two mortuary chapels.

Alterations and repairs were carried out to St Mary's Church costing about £2,000.

Work commenced on the reservoir on Wembdon Hill and water pipes were laid in Fore Street.

The Beehive Boot Depot, Eastover, advertised men's elastic side-boots from 5s. 6d. J. T. Rainforth, Fore Street, offered silver watches from one pound. Hooper & Co., St Mary Street, advertised sherry at 22s. per dozen bottles, and Bass's Ale, in 18-gallon casks, from 1s. 2d. per gallon.

The number of vessels entering the port was 3,864, totalling 233,039 tons.

The Mayor was Mr Thomas Collins.

1879 In May a fire escape was presented to the town by the Royal Society for the Protection of Life from Fire.

All the bells in St Mary's Church were refitted and rehung at a cost of £80.

A circus visited the town and a sensational part of the programme was the firing of a young lady into space from the muzzle of a cannon.

The vicarage of Holy Trinity Church in Taunton Road was built. The foundation stone was laid in April by the eldest daughter of the Rev George Trevor, the Vicar.

Tuesday, 2 December, was an important date in the history of Bridgwater when the official opening of the Bridgwater Corporation Waterworks took place. It was formally opened by the Mayor and Corporation amid much acclamation and was described as the largest and most important work by the Town Council of Bridgwater. The Waterworks were established at Ashford, Spaxton. The water was procured from various streams and filtered and pumped into a reservoir on Wembdon Hill. The occasion was made a public holiday and a great many people signified the satisfaction they felt on the completion of the work. The Mayor and Corporation and a large number of people dined at the Town Hall. During the afternoon an exhibition was given of fire-fighting. John Fackrell of the Fire Brigade rigged up a hydrant and a hose and turned on a stream, but the demonstration did not last long, for the weather was against it, as the water froze on the ground as it fell. It was a happy day; happy because the people realised that the old fear and dread of what a long, hot, rainless summer could do for them was gone for ever and water in abundance was always something to be thankful for!

A gallon of whisky was 18s.; a pair of the very best wool blankets 12s. 11d.; tea was 1s. 4d. a lb.; a 2lb. rich fruit cake could be bought for 2s.; tins of biscuits were 1s. 6d. A gallon of brandy cost 28s.; sherry was from 22s. per dozen bottles. Best cured ham cost 7d. a lb; cheese 6½d.; bacon 4½d. per lb.; and a quart jar of pickles 10½d. A good pair of strong working men's boots cost 7s. 6d.; women's best spring-sided boots cost 4s. 6d.; they were made of good honest leather—

indeed they needed to be, for Bridgwater's streets were either cobbled or thick with mud, churned up by the wheels of hansom cabs and broughams.

The Mayor, Mr W. T. Holland, had a daughter born unto him, and as this event happened in his year of office, it was resolved, according to the ancient custom of the borough, to present his worship with a silver cradle. A subscription was got up between the members of the Corporation, the magistrates of the Borough and the borough officers for the purchase of a suitable present. The so-called cradle consisted of a massive silver centrepiece engraved with a cradle, with the Borough arms on one side. The inscription engraved at the base of the piece was as follows: 'Presented to W. T. Holland Esq., by the aldermen, members of the Town Council and borough magistrates of the borough of Bridgwater, in commemoration of the birth of a daughter during his mayoralty. August 1879'. In the evening the Mayor was invited to a banquet at the *Royal Clarence* hotel and the presentation was made by the ex-Mayor, Mr T. Collins, on behalf of the subscribers.

The Bridgwater Christy Band was formed in this year.

The number of vessels entering the port was 4,089 of a total of 342,915 tons.

1880 Bridgwater in the 1880s was very much different from what it is today; drastic changes in the mode of living and national life have been brought about by wireless, television, the motor car, the cinema, and the aeroplane.

The main part of the town is still as it was in the 1800s, but the building of the Blake Bridge and Broadway has undoubtedly relieved the traffic congestion. In the 1880s the town was compact and from the centre one could almost say it was possible to throw a stone into the surrounding fields; but now approached from any direction there are suburbs, perhaps built to house workers in newly-introduced industries. St John Street, Eastover, Fore Street, High Street, and the Cornhill are the same except for new shops and businesses.

Bridgwater was more Liberal than Conservative but the scale was always turned by the rural voters, and thus the election meetings in the town were very lively.

With regard to religion, the town had three churches and in 1882 the Mission Church of All Saints and the Roman Catholic Church were opened. The Non-conformists of every denomination had Chapels in the town. The coming of the Salvation Army was in the 1880s. Their first efforts met with great opposition and meetings and marches were broken up, but they persisted, and now are recognised as a power for good.

During the 1880s small English towns such as Bridgwater were always well provided with Mayors who did their job well. They were usually businessmen and every year one was found to carry on the work which in some years might practically be a full-time occupation. Some even held the position for several years.

In the 1880s children were educated at Dr. Morgan's School (boarding and day), or at a small school in Dampiet Street. Elementary education was at St John's, West Street, St Mary's (girls), Eastover School, or Albert Street School.

The banks in Bridgwater were three 'local' ones. The Wilts and Dorset, Stuckeys, and Fox, Fowler & Co.

The industries of the town comprised the brick and tile trade and the famous manufacture of Bath bricks. The brickyards were all around the town and were sometimes called by the name of their locality, such as Dunwear, Hamp, or Somerset Bridge, and sometimes from the names of the owners, such as Brown's, Major's, or Symon's.

A flourishing foundry called Murch & Culverwell's carried on business in Eastover on the site where the Bridgwater Motor Company's premises are now. Messrs Roberts had a large coachbuilding business at No 27 Eastover. Shipbuilders and repairers were situated on the banks of the river–Gough's and Carver's being two of the firms so engaged. The timber trade employed a number of hands. Collar and shirt factories were started which gave occupation to female labour.

There are few survivals of the old shopkeepers, and old-fashioned grocers such as Backwell, Parsons, Lee and Soper are no longer to be found. Ironmongers such as Shrimpton & Halson have vanished, but Thompson's still carries on. Another way in which trade was carried on in the 1880s was by packmen, or travelling tradesmen, or 'Johnny Fortnightlies' as they were called. These went out from the town carrying packs of goods, usually clothing of various kinds, which they sold to cottagers in the country. These were often paid for by instalments and the money was called for every fortnight–hence the dealers' name. Usually they were Scotsmen. The more prosperous ones did their journeys in pony traps.

Another way of doing trade was by 'cheap jacks'. These men came to Bridgwater and some of them hired a yard just off Penel Orlieu. They sometimes stayed for weeks at a time and they sold all manner of goods–clocks, watches, vases, and other ornaments, and plated ware–all by a kind of auction. They sometimes drew large audiences, and to attract people held competitions for singing and step-dancing, for which prizes were given.

St Matthew's Fair was an outstanding occurrence held on the last Wednesday and Thursday in September. The Wednesday was primarily for the sale of stock, and horses, ponies, cattle and sheep changed hands by the hundreds.

Side by side with this was the pleasure fair with the tremendous din of the organs of several roundabouts all blaring forth different tunes. Shows, boxing booths and stands for the sale of sweets and gingerbreads were also there in great numbers. Thousands came to the Fair both for business and pleasure and West Street, which led to the Fairfield, was always crowded and lively.

Amusements were not much in evidence, an occasional concert in the Town Hall or the newly-opened Halswell Hall, and some short visits by theatrical companies were the extent of entertainment provided. Sport was well provided for and Bridgwater was famous for rugby football–the town providing many county players as well as a few internationals. Association football and cricket were popular. Cycling on penny-farthings was another kind of sport carried on with enthusiasm; and athletic sports were then very popular too.

Food and clothes were much cheaper, and alcoholic drinks and tobacco were incomparably cheaper. Income tax was a few pence in the pound, and wages were much lower.

In Bridgwater in the 1880s the Borough Policemen had beards and paraded the streets armed with canes which, incidentally, were used to good effect on youngsters who caused trouble.

In February the weather was so severe that it was possible to cross the river on the ice at a point near Saltlands.

In June a meeting of the inhabitants of the town was held to consider the advisability of the Midlands and London and South Western Railway Companies extending their joint lines to Bridgwater so as to increase passenger and goods traffic and provide the advantages resulting from railway competition.

The number of vessels entering the port was 3,677 of a total of 216,282 tons.

In this year the Salvation Army commenced operations in the town led by Captain Tom Crocker of Bristol. His first appearance as he walked through the streets singing and playing an accordian caused no little interest. The Army at first met with considerable opposition, which at one time appeared likely to be of a serious character, as a mob on one occasion besieged their meeting place and smashed the windows.

The Mayor was Mr William Thomas Holland.

1881 The Bridgwater Bicycle Club was formed.

A large number of ships used the port of Bridgwater—3,664 vessels with a total tonnage of over 204,000.

The River Parrett was frozen over this winter and people played a football match on the ice opposite the Lions, West Quay. Fires were lit on the frozen river.

The population of the town was 12,704.

At a meeting of the Town Council in August it was resolved that every facility should be given to the Bath and West of England Society and the Southern Counties Association to hold its annual meeting for 1883 in Bridgwater.

The Mayor was Mr Clifford Symons.

1882 The Roman Catholic Church, fronting the river in Binford Place, dedicated to St Joseph, was erected; it is an edifice of red brick and Bath stone in the Early Decorated style, and consists of chancel, nave of four bays, sacristy and a north aisle with a chapel at the east end. Many of the windows are stained and are memorials to the founder and to members of the York family. All Saints' Church, Westonzoyland Road, was built as a mission church for St John's. The building is now used by the Bridgwater Boys' Club.

St John's Church in Blake Place, was restored and afforded seating for 500 persons.

An Act of Parliament was obtained to allow of the formation of the Bridgwater and Edington Railway, in spite of the opposition of The Great Western Railway. The object of the Bill was 'to put Bridgwater in connection with the larger systems of the South Western Railway and the Midland Railway to which the Somerset and Dorset line forms in the direction of Bath on the one hand and of Templecombe on the other'.

The first organised Carnival procession took place this year.

A White Ribbon Army was formed in the town under the generalship of the Rev W. Highman, Pastor of the Bible Christian Chapel.

Changes were made at Bridgwater railway station and £3,700 was spent on the project. The platforms were extended by 15ft., glazed roofs were put over the platforms, and waiting rooms and a new footbridge connecting the two platforms was built.

The Mayor was Mr Thomas Collins, who died in office, followed by Mr R. O. Backwell.

1883 The 5 November was an auspicious occasion when the new Town Bridge was officially opened. By 1882 the old iron bridge had become inadequate for the ever-increasing traffic passing through the town, and it was not deemed strong enough to carry extra transport which would be occasioned by the visit of the Bath and West show to the town in 1883. A proposal to widen the old bridge fell through and the Corporation decided to replace it by a more modern structure. It was hoped that it would be ready for the Show, but high water caused by floods rendered difficult initial construction work, and it was not finished until October 1883. The tender of Mr George Moss of Liverpool amounting to £3,214 was accepted towards the close of 1882 for building the bridge and it was stipulated that the new bridge should be ready by 1 May 1883. It was described as 'an undertaking remarkable if only for the fact that its provision was accomplished without the necessity of increasing the rate of the Borough'. Ninety-three tons of wrought iron and 15 tons of cast iron were used in its making. Many inhabitants obtained pieces of the ironwork of the old bridge as souvenirs, the most interesting relic being acquired by Alderman J. Leaker, proprietor of the *Royal Clarence* hotel; it was the plaque commemorating the opening in 1795.

The new bridge was opened with true Victorian ceremony and pomp. The Mayoress, Mrs W. T. Holland, performed the ceremony. The Mayor, unfortunately, was unable to be present owing to a sharp attack of gout. The Mayoress was presented with a silver key (subscribed for by members of the Corporation) by the Town Clerk (Mr James Cook jnr) and she opened a padlock affixed to a brass chain suspended across the bridge. As soon as this obstruction was removed and the bridge declared open, Captain Barham, in command of the Bridgwater Rifle Corps, called upon his men to present arms, and the national anthem was sung. The various organisations and bodies in the town joined in the procession through the streets headed by the band of the Rifle Corps, under Mr Bradbeer. A well-attended luncheon followed in the Town Hall.

The bells of St Mary's Church rang at intervals during the day, and after the opening the workmen engaged in the construction of the bridge were given an excellent dinner of roast beef and plum pudding by the engineer, Mr Else. In the evening the bridge was again opened bv the annual Guy Fawkes Procession and received a 'Baptism of Fire'.

It is a matter of interest, as well as a tribute to the engineer engaged, that the present Town Bridge, built so many years ago to carry nothing more weighty than the horse-drawn vehicles, now carries massive amounts of traffic with apparently little strain.

The Boys' Brigade was founded in the town.

The years between 1880 and 1885 were the peak period for shipping in the port of Bridgwater, mostly of schooners and ketches. An average of more than 3,600 ships came annually, chiefly from ports in the Bristol Channel, carrying coal, timber, grain and sand, and taking away large quantities of bricks and tiles. The opening of road and rail services saw a falling off in trade, and in the late 1920s the number of ships was only about five hundred and thirty per annum. There is a tradition, apparently true, that the first ship to sight the Armada in the Bay of Biscay (1588) was sailing for Bridgwater. On arrival in England the Master immediately sent the news to Sir John Popham at Wellington.

The premises of the *Bridgwater Mercury* at the corner of Fore Street and Court Street were the scene of a disastrous fire.

The Mayor was Mr W. T. Holland.

1884 When rebuilding operations were going on behind Messrs Hook's Golden Key Grocery Warehouse in Fore Street, workmen made the interesting discovery of a portion of the old moat of Bridgwater Castle, which was filled with black mud and refuse.

The Somerset Agricultural Society was formed.

The Salvation Army was visited by General Booth, the leader of that organisation. The friendly greeting accorded to him was in marked contrast to the reception given to Mr Charles Bradlaugh, M.P. of Northampton, who, on coming to the Town Hall to lecture on 'Pensions', was pelted with rotten eggs and other filth and driven from the platform without being permitted to speak.

A great storm swept over the town on 25 and 26 January causing much damage. The roof of St John's Church was badly damaged and two windows were blown in.

The Mayor was Mr Francis James Thompson, of the firm of ironmongers in the town. He was a strong temperance advocate and a Quaker and was held by everybody in the highest esteem. Mr Edward J. Stanley of Quantock Lodge became Conservative M.P.

1885 On 8 January, the day Prince Albert came of age, there was a public demonstration in honour of the event. All the aged people in the town were treated to a substantial dinner in the Market House, and those unable to attend due to the inclement weather, and the sick and the infirm, had dinners sent to them in their homes. The Mayor sent a congratulatory telegram to the Prince, which was afterwards duly acknowledged.

A handsome and commodious reading room and library was opened in High Street. It was regarded as a boon to the inhabitants.

At the General Election held on 8 December the result was as follows:

Mr E. J. Stanley (Conservative)	3,935
Mr Trevillian (Liberal)	3,835

(Conservative majority, 100)

This was the first election of Bridgwater as a county division since the Bridgwater Borough was disenfranchised in 1869. The constituency returned one Member to Parliament.

On Saturday, 11 July, the newspaper called *The Bridgwater Independent* was established by James Bulgin. It was published in Bridgwater and printed in York Buildings. After a year it was sold to Messrs Whitby and Sons, Cornhill. It later passed to Mr Harry Law, who owned a number of other papers in Somerset, and from him to Mr C. H. Mills. The copyright of this paper was acquired by *The Bridgwater Mercury* in June 1933 and incorporated in that newspaper.

A newspaper called *The Bridgwater Guardian* was established. It was published at Bridgwater at the offices of the former *Bridgwater Gazette* in George Street. Its existence was a brief one.

The Bridgwater Dramatic Society was formed in this year.

The Mayor was Mr Alfred Peace.

1886 In the General Election held on 7 July, Mr E. J. Stanley (Conservative) was returned unopposed as M.P. for Bridgwater.

The Jubilee of the Temperance League was celebrated in Bridgwater on 19 August with much enthusiasm. The proceedings included a well-attended meeting at the Town Hall, and a tea at the Friends' Meeting House.

The Bridgwater shipping trade suffered a big blow with the opening of the Severn Tunnel.

A good deal of distress prevailed in the town during a strike on the part of the brickyard workers; about one hundred of them remained out of work for several weeks.

An important improvement took place with the repairing of the dock gates and the cleansing of the docks and canal.

The Parrett Bath Brick Company and a collar factory were started as new industries in the town.

The Mayor was Mr Alfred Garrett Barham.

1887 On Monday, 20 June the Jubilee of Queen Victoria was celebrated. The occasion was marked in Bridgwater and throughout the neighbourhood with every demonstration of loyalty. Some months previous to the day a representative town committee was appointed and the question as to how the Jubilee might best be commemorated was earnestly discussed. It was then agreed that an effort should be made to mark the occasion by establishing public baths in the Borough, the cost to be provided by public subscription. Alderman F. J. Thompson generously offered £100 towards the cost, but the public appeal for subscriptions was so disappointing in its result that the proposal had to be abandoned. It was then agreed that the funds should be spent in a general demonstration. There was a grand procession through the town, including the Mayor and Corporation, Rifle Volunteers, three bands, The West Somerset Yeomanry, Cavalry, Magistrates, Fire Brigades, Friendly Societies, and general inhabitants, and all attended a special Service at St Mary's Church, which was crowded.

Those taking part in the procession afterwards assembled on the Cornhill where the national anthem was sung by the multitude, and the Volunteers fired a *feu de joie.* At 1 p.m. a free dinner was provided at the Market House for 700 poor persons over 60 years of age. About half a ton of beef and mutton was cooked, and about the same weight of potatoes. A great number of plum puddings were kindly given by residents of the town.

Over 3,000 children of the town were provided with tea in Mr J. H. Waddon's Rope Walk. Afterwards, and to their great joy, they played various games. They were also presented with commemoration medals, as were many who did not attend the celebrations, and the total number of medals distributed was about four thousand. In the afternoon a public fête took place at Blacklands at which some 2,000 people were present. A variety of entertainment was much enjoyed and a military tournament attracted much interest. The day's proceedings passed off most successfully.

Some repairs were carried out to St. Mary's Church tower and spire, and a small scaffold was erected on the summit. An enterprising townsman, Mr. J. S. Brown, mounted the ladders with a camera and took an interesting photograph of the town looking down Fore Street.

The Somerset Agricultural Association held their first show at Bridgwater.

On 15 May a Bridgwater centenarian named Sarah Tapson died in a ward in Chelsea Workhouse, having reached the age of one hundred and eight.

Suits to measure were from 27s. 6d.; wedding rings (22 carat) were from 10s.; the best tea at 2s. a lb.; and good strong working-men's boots from 4s. 11d. a pair (which were obtainable from Albert Lewis, High Street, who also sold shoes for infants at sixpence a pair).

If one wanted to 'get ahead', then Simmonds & Co., Fore Street, were the people who sold hats. In Eastover, J. Sanders repaired clocks and watches while, also in Eastover, there was Tytherleigh's where a really good overcoat cost only 25s. Bridgwater sausages and Bath polonies were made at the St Mary Street shop of W. R. Poole, and in the same street Bouchiers, the furnishers, traded under the motto 'Small profits, quick returns'.

The George William Memorial Hall constituting the new headquarters of the Young Men's Christian Association was formally opened on 16 October.

A football match was played on the frozen River Parrett, opposite The Lions, West Quay. People of all ages revelled on the ice-bound river and on the brickyard ponds.

A long red streamer was flown from the top of St Mary's Church spire in honour of Queen Victoria's Jubilee.

The Bridgwater Guy Fawkes Carnival was celebrated on 7 November. The customary bonfire on the Cornhill was set alight, and iron fencing, specially constructed, was used because of complaints that the excessive heat, and the size of the fire, was dangerous. There was also a smaller bonfire on the Pig Cross in front of the Cattle Market. It had been announced that the procession would traverse West Quay, Castle Street and the Square, but owing to the drainage works then in progress on West Quay that part of the route had to be abandoned. After the Christy Band played the national anthem, the fun of the evening commenced, and the streets were full of minstrel troupes playing and singing, and squibs were discharged. Almost before it was dark some of the shopkeepers made their usual preparations for the safety of their premises. On the Cornhill and Fore Street the shop windows were protected either by boards placed across the front, or sacking.

A handsome and costly gold chain and badge of office was provided by subscriptions for the use of all future Mayors of the town on 'State' occasions. The chain consisted of one centre and 18 ordinary links with pendant and badge. It cost £170.

The pinnacles were added to the tower of St John's Church. The whole of the cost was defrayed by the Rev N. H. Ruddock.

The Mayor was Mr Alfred Peace.

1888 A movement was inaugurated in London for the purpose of providing a memorial to the celebrated Admiral Blake. The idea was well taken up, and St Margaret's, Westminster, was enriched with a stained glass window. It has three large figure subjects, surmounted by canopies wholly in silver white glass, with ruby backgrounds. The inscription beneath the window runs as follows:

> To the Glory of God and to the Memory of Colonel Robert Blake, Admiral at Sea and chief founder of England's Naval supremacy died August the 7th 1657—disinterred from his grave in the Abbey and re-buried in St. Margaret's church, 1661.

The project of constructing a ship canal between Bridgwater Bay and the English Channel, first considered in 1825, was again brought forward, though it was difficult to predict the chances of its ever being brought to pass.

The Mayor was Mr William Hurman.

1889 Monday, 1 April, was the official inauguration of the Somerset County Council. There was a contest for two representatives for Bridgwater, and Mr F. J. Thompson and Mr W. L. Winterbotham were elected.

On Friday, 8 March, floods occurred in the town and district owing to the rapid thaw of deep snow.

A bronze bust of Queen Victoria was placed in the Town Hall.

Mr William Browne presented the Unitarian Chapel with a new organ.

The number of vessels entering the port was 2,932 of a total of 186,942 tons.

Mr S. G. Jarman's *History of Bridgwater* was published. It is a very comprehensive and ably-written work, and much credit must be given to its painstaking author. The inhabitants are indebted to Mr. Jarman for furnishing such a complete and reliable history of the borough.

The Mayor was Mr John Henry Waddon.

1890 In March there was a strike when 500-600 brickyard workers remained out for three weeks.

The Bridgwater Club, now known as the County Club, was formed in King Square in this year.

On 1 August Mr E. J. Stanley, M.P., formally opened the new swimming baths described as one of the largest which were in the west of England. It was constructed by Mr H. W. Pollard at the expense of the Rev Father Scoles, whose public spirit in providing the town requirement was warmly commended.

The construction of the railway from Bridgwater to Edington on the Somerset and Dorset railway line, by means of which Bridgwater would be placed in direct communication with the Midland & South Western systems, proceeded during the year.

In July, on a very wet day, the Somerset & Dorset railway station was officially opened. The streets of Bridgwater were bedecked with flags in honour of the occasion which it was hoped would bring prosperity to the town. Because of the downpour, a civic reception which was to have greeted the first train had to be abandoned.

The following notice appeared in the town in December:

> Notice is hereby given that two soup kitchens will be opened on Thursday next the 1 January 1891 between the hours of 11.30 and 1 o'clock. The kitchen for the western district will be at Mr Bellringer's, the *Blake Arms* (entrance from Fryern Street) and the kitchen for the eastern district will be at Mrs Lovibond's at the corner of Monmouth Street and Blake Place. Both kitchens will, for the present, be open on Tuesday, Thursday and Saturday of each week between the hours of 11.30 and 1 o'clock. Tickets for the soup and bread, price one penny, can be obtained from: Mr T. J. Barton, Chemist, Cornhill; Mr J. A. Basker, Chemist, Fore Street; Mr L. H. Llewellyn, Chemist, Penel Orlieu; Mr Wm. Bouchier, the Eastover Stores; Mr Wm. Hickman, Chemist, Eastover; and Mr Wm. Perrett, Grocer, St John Street. Dated Bridgwater, 30 December 1890.

The Mayor was Mr Frederick C. Foster.

1891 The population of the town was 12,419.

The number of vessels entering the port was 2,648 of a total of 166,768 tons.

The Mayor was Mr Henry Knight.

1892 The broad gauge on the Great Western Railway was discontinued.

In April the Sunday School and Parish Room of Holy Trinity Church was opened by the Mayor and Corporation; the building cost about six hundred pounds.

The number of vessels entering the port had fallen from 3,330 in 1890 to 2,531 in 1892, a decrease of 799 vessels in two years (the decreased tonnage amounted to 30,000 tons). The explanation for this was that most of the coal traffic from South Wales had been diverted through the Severn Tunnel and that the railway rates then in force operated very judicially to the interest of the port.

At the General Election held in this year the result was as follows:

Mr E. J. Stanley (Conservative)	4,555
Mr F. Walker (Liberal)	3,362

(Conservative majority, 1,193)

Improvements were made to many municipal buildings including the Council Chambers, and the erection of a master's residence contiguous to the Albert Street Board School. At the upper end of St Mary Street, Mr Squibbs, auctioneer, had finished building some commodious business premises and the Collegiate School.

The Medical Health Officer, Dr F. J. C. Parsons reported an unusually heavy death rate of not less than 31.6 per thousand, which he attributed almost entirely to the severity of the influenza epidemic.

On the night of 26 February a great fire occurred at the Oil and Cake Mills of Messrs Croad & Brown at the Docks.

The Mayor was Mr Thomas W. Manchip.

1893 Monday, 21 August, marked the official re-opening of the town's Public Baths in Old Taunton Road. There was a colourful civic procession to and from the Town Hall with the pealing of the Church bells. In early 1893 the Baths were acquired by Councillor W. H. Roberts, who had a carriage works in Eastover, and he offered them to the Corporation on certain conditions. So it came about that the Town Council officially took responsibility for the Baths on 21 August of that year.

Very satisfactory arrangements were made for holding a Mayoral Banquet in the Town Hall. This was the first occasion that such a function had taken place and it was hoped that it would be held every succeeding year.

The Committee of the Guy Fawkes Carnival contemplated building a fireworks factory, where fireworks could be made in accordance with legal requirements. Negotiations were started with a view to the purchase of land and various sites near the Docks were inspected, and the possibility of adapting a building in Taunton Road as such a factory was also considered. The project never materialised. In 1893 the Guy Fawkes Carnival was revived.

In March a local branch of the District Nursing Association was formed in Bridgwater. The Hon Mrs Stanley accepted the office of Lady President and an influential committee of ladies was appointed.

Superintendent Lear, who had previously been the recipient of a handsome testimonial, was paid a graceful and well-deserved compliment by the Bridgwater Corporation when it unanimously accepted a resolution congratulating him on the satisfactory completion of more than half a century's service to the borough in connection with the Police Force and his retirement into private life with a superannuation allowance.

A Ratepayers' Association was formed in the town to keep a more watchful eye on public expenditure.

In May the majority of bricklayers in the town went on strike because their employers refused to concede their demand for one penny per hour extra.

It was reported to a meeting of the Guardians of the Poor that there was a great increase in the number of tramps in Bridgwater. Sixty-one had been admitted to the workhouse in one week.

It was suggested that a new Bridgwater to Minehead road should be built to avoid the dangers of Wembdon Hill.

The number of vessels entering the port was 2,737 of a total of 149,282 tons.

The Mayor was Mr Henry William Pollard.

1894 The Corporation of Bridgwater were busily engaged in the consideration of many schemes affecting the town's welfare and chief amongst them was the revival of the proposal for the construction of a ship canal. The Mayor, Mr. H. W. Pollard, availed himself of the first opportunity to support the suggestion and was backed up by influential townspeople.

The scheme was first presented to the Corporation in 1835 by Mr Price. Ultimately it was agreed to offer prizes, one of 100 guineas and a second of 25 guineas, for the best schemes 'For the improvement of the navigation of the port either by means of a ship canal or otherwise, together with an estimate of the cost'.

The most noteworthy event in Bridgwater during the year was the ninth annual exhibition of the Somerset Agricultural Association in May, when prizes of about £1,200 were awarded. The Show was a highly successful one and very largely attended, notwithstanding the inclement weather. Its success was largely contributed to by the indefatigable exertions of the Hon Secretary (Mr T. H. Boys) and the influential attendance on the first day, when the members of the Council and a large number of gentlemen attended a luncheon, by invitation of the Mayor, who generously provided it.

A violent thunderstorm occurred on 26 May and the spire of St Mary's Church was struck and damaged by lightning. During the storm's progress a seaman named John Bennett was instantly killed at Pounds Fields, and a Captain who was by his side was hurled into a ditch and rendered unconscious.

A Prize Fat Stock Show was held at the Market for the first time shortly before Christmas, and was attended with so much success as to ensure its continuance in future years.

The number of vessels entering the port was 2,359 of a total of 147,015 tons.

1895 On 2 January the Bridgwater Rural District Council was first established. It covered the area of the Rural Sanitary Authority and 39 of the 44 Councillors attended the first meeting. At the time there was one representative for each parish with the exception of Puriton which, for some unknown reason, had failed to return a councillor. The Council then met fortnightly and were concerned with roads and public health matters. The first Chairman was the Rev G. C. Anderson of Otterhampton, and the Vice-Chairman was Mr G. E. Lansdowne of Over Stowey. The late Rev P. T. Pryce-Mitchell became the Vice-Chairman in the same year and eventually succeeded Mr Lansdowne in 1930. He held the office until 1945, a total service of over half a century.

On 24 March the ketch *Active* foundered off Burnham at the tail of the Gore and notwithstanding the efforts of the lifeboat crew to rescue them, all the crew were drowned. Another ship, the *Hereford* of Bridgwater, foundered in a fearful gale and all the crew were drowned, whilst the *Tender,* a tug from Bridgwater, capsized off Burnham Pier and the engineer, George Harding, was drowned.

At the General Election held 15 July, Mr E. J. Stanley (Conservative) was returned unopposed.

The railings were removed from around the Cornhill on 20 September by order of the Market Buildings Committee of the Bridgwater Corporation.

The River Parrett was frozen over for a considerable time during the hard winter of 1895.

The number of vessels entering the port was 2,303 of a total of 142,337 tons.

The Mayor was Mr Henry William Pollard.

1896 The borough of Bridgwater was enlarged when portions of the parishes of Bridgwater without and Wembdon were added.

A serious strike of workers engaged in the brickmaking industry occurred. Mr Richard Else was at length nominated as arbitrator in the dispute, but the situation was so serious that rioting began, and soldiers from Plymouth had to be drafted into the town, and lodged in temporary quarters within the Town Hall. On 3 July at 3 a.m., the Mayor read the Riot Act, directing all the people to disperse peaceably and return to their homes. Thus quiet was restored, but the strike had lasted 14 weeks and much distress had been caused.

The town's biggest blaze occurred in November at Robert's Carriage Works situated at the junction of New Road and Eastover.

The number of vessels entering the port was 2,338 of a total of 149,390 tons.

The Mayor was Mr Richard Charles Else.

1897 The spire of St Mary's Church was ascended and repairs were made to the damage caused by lightning in 1894.

The premises known as the 'Perseverance Works' were erected by Messrs W. & F. Wills. They were well worth inspection, as they illustrated the latest type of well-arranged and thoroughly-ventilated workshops.

The laying of the foundation stone of the new Post Office on the Cornhill took place this year.

The erection of a commodious factory by the Tone Vale Manufacturing Co., who had already spent about £7,000 in this local industry, afforded profitable employment to a large number of people.

A branch railway was extended by the G.W.R. to Messrs Starkey, Knight & Ford's premises at Northgate.

In the suburbs of Bridgwater a large number of new houses, especially small villas, were built, most of which found occupants almost immediately.

The Lighting Committee of the Bridgwater Corporation decided to apply for the necessary Parliamentary authorisation to install electric instead of gas lighting in the principal thoroughfares of the town, at an estimated cost of £15,000.

The number of vessels entering the port was 2,403 of a total of 155,170 tons.

There was a town bus service from Wembdon to the railway station, with one-penny stages at the Bridge and the Cemetery. There were cabstands in High Street (one opposite the Town Hall and the other near the Produce Market) Penel Orlieu, Salmon Parade, and the entrance to the railway station yard. Royal Mail omnibuses plied between Bridgwater and Kilve, a journey of 2¾ hours, costing 1s. 3d., and between Bridgwater and Glastonbury, a journey of three hours costing 1s. 6d.

The population had grown to 14,000.

The last house in Bristol Road was No. 140, No. 129 in Bath Road. The *Hope* inn was almost the last building in Taunton Road, but Road Lane (note the spelling) had 14 cottages and a few houses. There were 18 cottages in Hamp Ward, and 18 in Honeysuckle Alley. There were no fewer than 18 courts in West Street with a total of 89 cottages, and there were more than 80 cottages in the courts of Albert Street. St John Street had 12 inns, among them the *Sailor's Home,* the *Beehive* and the *Steam Packet* inn. Barclay Street had the *Bell* inn, and the *Barclay Arms* inn. St Mary Street had the *Alexandra* hotel; Mansion House Lane had the *Shipwright's Arms*; Binford Place had the *Dolphin* inn and the *Castle* inn.

The town had a Ratepayers' and Owners' Protection Association, a Sailors' Rest, a Y.M.C.A., more than two dozen Friendly Societies, a Teetotal Club, a Teetotal Society, and several other temperance organisations.

Letters posted at Bridgwater at 1.30 p.m. were delivered in London the same evening at 9.15 p.m.

The Mayor was Mr Frederick C. Foster.

1898 The West Bow improvement, the widening of the corner at the bottom of West Street, was effected by the purchase and removal of some houses at the junction of North Street and Penel Orlieu. It was hoped that this might be the means of preventing the many serious accidents that occurred at this dangerous corner.

Very favourable consideration was given by the Bridgwater Rural District Council to a proposal to construct a light railway from Bridgwater to Othery, via Westonzoyland and Middlezoy.

Binford House was purchased by Bridgwater Corporation in this year.

A public subscription list was opened with the object of presenting the town with a statue of Bridgwater's greatest hero, Admiral Robert Blake.

The number of vessels entering the port was 2,096 of a total of 134,098 tons.

Bridgwater Steeplechase and Hurdle Races were re-established under National Hunt Rules. The course was a fine grass one, over a mile round with a natural grandstand in the centre, accommodating over 3,000 people.

In August four local businessmen made up their minds to spend a week's holiday together on a driving tour through the West Country. Notes of the journey were made by Mr T. H. Boys, auctioneer and estate agent. The other three travellers were Frederick Boys, John Richards, and Richard Popham. It was stated by the writer that it was not often that four businessmen, always active in their respective capacities, could find time to take a lengthy holiday. A day once now and then they may manage, but when it comes to a week or ten days continually, clean away from the trammels of their respective callings, some little hesitation is experienced before their minds are thoroughly made up to relinquish the monotonous cares of a busy life. However, all anxieties were cast aside when the four gentlemen consulted with each other, and after discussing various necessary preliminaries determined to abandon, for at least a week, the daily toil of business pursuits and enjoy an uninterrupted holiday. One of the party was selected as 'cashier', and he was to pay all expenses of the journey, to be divided into four on its completion.

The manager of the Bridgwater Cab and Posting Company provided a capital turnout of a most comfortable landau; a pair of spanking horses; a steady coachman, courteous and obliging, and a very careful driver, who managed his horses in a masterly manner. They started from Bridgwater at 9.30 on the morning of Friday, 19 August in the brightest of weather. The route of the tour through Somerset and Devon included Minehead, Dunster, Timberscombe, Barnstaple, Woolacombe, Ilfracombe, Combe Martin, Lynton, Lynmouth, Exford, Simonsbath, Dulverton, Wiveliscombe, Milverton, Cothelstone to Enmore, and home to Bridgwater. The journey was described very fully, with accounts of where they stayed and the accommodation and meals provided, and the sites, views and experiences encountered. The trip was most enjoyable, being favoured with fine weather, although at times the heat was almost tropical. The day after the return the accounts were made up and everything settled to the satisfaction and pleasure of all. The travellers were left with many pleasant memories of the most enjoyable week's outing they had ever experienced.

The Mayor was Mr Thomas Good.

1899 The restoration and re-hanging of St Mary's Church bells was completed at an expense of £500, obtained by subscription. The dedication ceremony took place in October, and the service was attended by the Mayor and Corporation in 'state' procession.

In March, 21 Bridgwater volunteers left for active service in the Boer War in South Africa.

Henry J. Prince, founder of the Agapemone, died.

The rejection of the scheme did not deter the promoters of the proposed light railway from Bridgwater to Stogursey from publishing notice of their intended application for power to construct a railway from the eastern side of the Parrett and underneath the river by a tunnel through Wembdon, Cannington and on to Nether Stowey and Stogursey. As the undertaking had influential backing there was good reason to hope for a satisfactory result.

The Lighting Committee of the Borough Council adopted by eight votes to six a motion to light the borough with electricity, though this did not actually come into effect until 1904.

Mr. William Catlow of St Albyn's School, Dulwich, received the appointment of Headmaster of Dr Morgan's School, vacated by the Rev C. E. Lucette, who had accepted the Headmastership of Chard Grammar School.

In July a violent thunderstorm visited the neighbourhood, and at Westonzoyland the destructive effects of a pitiless hailstorm accompanying the storm were so great that from £1,200 to £1,500 worth of damage was caused to grown crops, fruit trees, and house property.

The number of vessels entering the port was 2,320 of a total of 146,502 tons.

The Mayor was Mr Thomas Good.

1900 At the General Election held on 1 October, Mr E. J. Stanley (Conservative) was returned unopposed.

The unveiling of the statue to Admiral Robert Blake took place on Thursday, 4 October.

On 18 May enthusiastic festivities were held to celebrate the relief of Ladysmith and Mafeking.

The number of vessels entering the port was 2,057 of a total of 131,884 tons.

The Mayor was Mr William Thompson.

1901 Sugar could be bought in Bridgwater for 1s. 6d. for 12lbs. Tea could be bought for 7d. a lb. at the Golden Key in Fore Street. At Lewis's on the Cornhill, men's boots were being sold at 3s. 9d. a pair, and ladies' dress shoes at 1s. a pair. Finest dairy-fed pork cost only 5d. a lb. at Fred Hook's shop in Eastover. At *Crocker's Tavern* a penny would buy a cup of tea, coffee or cocoa.

The population of Bridgwater was 15,168.

Much satisfaction was expressed at the final approval by the Board of Trade for the Bridgwater and Stogursey light railway scheme; an undertaking, which, it was hoped, could be carried into effect during the coming year and prove very beneficial to the town and neighbourhood.

The lamented death of Her Majesty Queen Victoria was followed by well-attended memorial services in St Mary's Church and the Congregational Church. The proclamation of His Majesty, King Edward VII on the Cornhill by the Mayor, Councillor William Thompson, was followed by a vote of congratulation from the Corporation to His Majesty on his accession to the throne.

The number of vessels entering the port was 2,971 of a total of 170,654 tons.

1902 The year 1902 is chiefly memorable for the coronation of King Edward VII and the termination of the Boer War, both events being celebrated in Bridgwater in a befitting manner. Preparations in August for the coronation celebration had been on a very elaborate scale and were highly successful. The day's events had begun with the official opening of Blake Gardens by the Mayoress, Mrs T. W. Manchip; she performed the ceremony at the Dampiet Street entrance to the Gardens with a golden key handed to her by Alderman Pollard. Later, at the Old Taunton Road end of the Gardens, the Mayoress planted a commemoration oak—to grow as a 'living witness for generations'.

On the occasion of the Peace celebrations in June, Thanksgiving services were held in St Mary's Church and other places of worship, and the children were given a holiday.

The most important new industry established in Bridgwater was the cabinet manufacturing establishment erected by Mr H. J. Van Trump and Mr Humphrey, his son-in-law.

There was a sad shipping disaster off the coast of Wales when the ship *Halswell* foundered with the loss of her captain and crew belonging to Bridgwater.

The number of vessels entering the port was 3,147 of a total of 177,246 tons.

In Coronation year Bridgwater Guy Fawkes Carnival night took place on an elaborate scale. There were more gangs than for many years, a record number of masqueraders, and a magnificent tableau of the Royal Pageant at the Coronation of King Edward VII and Queen Alexandra. The royal procession was the first time that such a long series of connected tableaux had been attempted. The first carriage contained the ecclesiastical dignitories who had assisted at the Coronation. Then came a gorgeous stage coach, drawn by eight spanking cream-coloured horses, with the King and Queen in their Coronation robes, a-glitter with shining jewels. The handsome gilded coach was quite a close imitation of the original and in the torchlight and coloured fire illumination the effect was almost dazzling. There was the customary huge bonfire on the Cornhill. Overnight a consignment of fuel was deposited in front of the Market House Dome, and next day cartloads of material were continually arriving. There were tar barrels, an old boat, and wood of all descriptions in very large quantities. At intervals throughout the day rain had threatened to spoil the proceedings, but at about half-past-seven everybody experienced a great relief when the downpour ceased, and for the remainder of the night there was the best possible weather.

The Mayor was Mr Thomas William Manchip.

1903 In June an outing took place for Mr R. Moddy's Collar Factory workers to Holford and St Audries. The factory was in Dampiet Street, and about 180 people set off in five horse-drawn brakes supplied by Messrs Alpin & Son. It was a magnificent turnout and Mr A Squibbs, the photographer, was commissioned to photograph the scene on the Cornhill. Among the occupants of the first brake were several bandsmen who played lively music as the horses trotted along at a leisurely pace. The steep Wembdon Hill had to be negotiated and the occupants of the brakes had to get out and walk in order to ease the burden on the horses. The brakes were halted at Holford to allow the party to wander among the picturesque surroundings. It was a most enjoyable day with mountains of food, teapots of gargantuan size and mugs of foaming English ale. The homeward journey was the best part of the day, and the last stop before reaching Bridgwater was the *Plough,* Holford.

The Bridgwater Motor Company was formed and extensive new premises in Eastover were erected.

The Bridgwater Steam Laundry in Taunton Road was erected at a cost of £3,000 and was formally opened in May.

A new parcels office at the Great Western railway station was opened.

St Mary's Parish Hall, in King Square, was erected at a cost of £1,000, the whole being defrayed by public subscription. It was used for general parochial purposes.

The number of vessels entering the port was 2,975 of a total of 163,960 tons.

Tremendous interest was aroused, and increased daily, in a proposed race from Bristol to Bridgwater. When the great day arrived–Saturday, 20 June– the mood had developed into 'an intensity that almost bordered on the frantic'. The newspaper headline was 'The Great Walk, Bristol to Bridgwater. A magnificent and fast race. The favourite beaten. R. G. Carey wins grandly'. Carey received a silver cup awarded by the committee, and a marble clock presented by the proprietors of *The Mercury*. A son of the Rev Jabez Carey, Congregational minister at Puriton, he was an an assistant at the photographic studio of Mr A. Squibbs.

Praise was given to the admirable police arrangements made by Chief Constable Barnett and his staff. They were obliged to divert all traffic from Fore Street, 'which was literally thronged with people, while on the Cornhill the scene as viewed from the balconies and windows of the surrounding houses closely resembled that which the townspeople were familiar with about 30 years ago, when hustings were erected in front of the Market Place on the occasion of contested elections'.

Walking races were a great attraction and a great amount of interest was aroused by the pedestrian feats of this period.

The worst storm of the century was on the night of Thursday, 10 September. There was an exceptionally heavy rainfall and a terrific gale caused havoc, not only in the town and surrounding villages, but in almost every part of Somerset. The tide rose from 14ft. 4ins. to over 20ft., receded once, then came again in a second flow. The river quickly overflowed into Salmon Parade and Binford Place and, where barricades had not been erected, the houses were badly flooded. But it was the inhabitants of Old Taunton Road who had most cause for alarm, for they were totally unprepared, yet the murky water of the Parrett very soon found its way there. It extinguished fires at the Gas Works and kilns at a number of brickyards. Shipping in the docks and the river was not so badly affected as it might have been, though a 22-ton barge which had been moored at Somerset Bridge broke away and sank. For a time anxiety was felt for several Bridgwater vessels known to be at sea. In all parts of the town extensive damage was done by the gale, which brought down several trees, chimney pots and tiles. The Kilve mail cart was delayed and the driver had to try three different routes to reached Bridgwater Post Office.

A cab driver returning from Nether Stowey Sports found the roadway impassable, made a wide detour across the fields and succeeded in reaching Wembdon, but here again the road was barred by several large trees. The storm had a most disastrous effect upon the telephone and telegraph wires, and

Bridgwater was out of communication on Friday with nearly everywhere of importance save Taunton and Exeter. At the Malt Shovel Field–now Victoria Park–Mr Holloway's Pavilion of Varieties had been giving performances for some months, but it was decided not to give a performance on that memorable Thursday night, but to strengthen the stays. At about 10 o'clock the wind lifted the roof clean away, wrecking the structure which the unfortunate showman had been unable to insure. Three people were killed at Nether Stowey.

R. Squibbs & Son, auctioneers, valuers and house agents of 7 King Square announced that they had purchased the entire business of the Bridgwater Furnishing Co., Ltd., Cattle Market, Bridgwater. Among the costly stock on view in their extensive showrooms were bedroom suites from £5 10s. 0d.; parlour suites in leather from £3 5s. 0d.; walnut overmantles from 16s. 6d.; and marble-top washstands from 8s. 6d. Goods were supplied on the hire purchase system.

The Golden Key, Fore Street offered currants at 2d. per lb., dates at 4d. per lb., dates at 4d. per lb. and oranges at 3d. per dozen, Christmas puddings were 10½d. The Bank, High Street, proprietor W. M. Hook, offered pork sausages at 6d. per lb., finest quality 8d., Wiltshire smoked bacon 4½d to 10d. per lb. Every customer who spent not less than 1s. 6d. at Hickman's Drug Store, Eastover, received a large bottle of good port wine free, or if a teetotal, a bottle of the finest quality ginger wine. Dick's, St Mary Street, offered a range of ladies' shoes for parties and dances from 1s. 11½d. to 3s. 11d. Alway & Sons, the White Horse Stores offered Scotch and Irish whisky and rum, all at half-a-crown a bottle. Best Lydney coal was delivered to any part of the town at 22s. per ton. 'Seasonable lines' offered by Lee, grocer, 23 Dore Street, were peaches at 9½d. per tin, apricots at 8½d per tin, pineapple chunks at 7½d. per tin; and non-alcoholic wines in various flavours at 1s. 1½d per bottle. The Bridgwater Motor Co. offered cars for immediate delivery, with free trials to likely purchasers and free tuition to buyers: a secondhand 6 h.p. De Dion to carry four to five persons, £200; a 5 h.p. Decauville to carry three passengers, £80; a new 14 h.p. Daimler to carry five passengers £750; a 6 h.p. Argyll with bucket-seats to carry two passengers, £208. Flour was 12lb. for 1s. 2d.; 3lb. of ham was 1s. 3d.; tea was 1s. 4d. per lb.; nine tablets of toilet soap, 1s; oatmeal was 7lb. for 1s.; and lump sugar 2d. per lb.

The Mayor was Mr Thomas William Manchip.

1904 The old *Malt Shovel* hotel was pulled down and rebuilt.

The widening of the road leading to King Square at the entrance to York Buildings from the Cornhill was carried out.

The new railway bridge across the river at Somerset Bridge was completed.

At the Great Western railway station the platforms were extended and a new parcels office was provided, with a footbridge alongside.

Suits to measure were from £1 7s. 6d., with 10 per cent. off for cash; they were advertised by W. W. Baker & Co., of St Mary Street. Bacon was offered at 6½d. per lb by Mr Lee of Fore Street.

On 15 August General Booth, the Head of the Salvation Army, visited the town, and there was a big Salvation Army demonstration in the Town Hall, where he was welcomed by the Mayor, who presented him with an address. It was generally acknowledged that in Bridgwater the work of the Salvation Army produced good results.

Bridgwater had electric light for the first time. Early in the year it was announced that the Bridgwater and District Electric Supply and Traction Co., Ltd., had signed a contract for the erection of a generating station, producing house, and other necessary buildings. Eight tenders were received, and the entire cost, including all requisite plant and machinery, was said to exceed £20,000. Other ways of using electricity than for light and power were explained in a large display advertisement in *The Mercury* soon after the installation. A gentleman from High Holborn, London, styling himself as a 'medical electrician', announced that he would be attending at 28 Fore Street, for the treatment of disease by electricity.

Dosson Bros., the men's tailors of High Street, offered men's suits (usually £1 1s. 0d.) at 10s. 11d.; trousers at 2s. 6½d.; shirts at 1s. 6½d.; men's caps at 2½d.; boys' waterproofs (usually 15s. 6d.) at 6s. 11d.; youth's moleskin trousers, slightly spotted at 2s. 6d.; and umbrellas at 1s. 11½d. The tailoring department offered made-to-measure suits from £1 2s. 6d.

The Great Western Railway announced that express trains from Bridgwater to Paddington now took three and a half hours. Passenger's luggage could be collected and delivered in advance for 1s. per package. Hot or cold luncheons with a bottle of beer cost 3s., without beer 2s. 6d. Tea basket containing pot of tea or coffee, bread and butter, cake or bun cost 2s.

The number of vessels entering the port was 3,055 of a total of 189,494 tons.

The Mayor was Mr Henry William Pollard.

1905 An agitation was set on foot in favour of the abandonment or modification of the Guy Fawkes demonstration in the town. When Bridgwater Guy Fawkes Carnival was held this year it marked the 21st anniversary of the town's first properly organised Carnival. The Carnival of 1905 was held on Monday, 6 November, and according to a report of the proceedings, Monday was then recognised as a half holiday for local shops. Perhaps it was when early closing day moved to Thursday that the day of the Carnival changed also.

An attempt by the Bridgwater Corporation to improve navigation of the Parrett by the provision of an eroder, or scouring-boat, was the subject of a Board of Trade enquiry. The scheme was opposed by several ship owners and merchants, as well as by the Great Western Railway which owned the Docks, and resulted in the absolute rejection of the scheme.

In this year there was continued growth and prosperity in the town, completely justifying the familiar and oft-used phrase 'Progressive Bridgwater'. Particularly remarkable was the expansion that took place in the suburbs where newly-built villas and rows of new houses were springing up in almost every direction.

Two new roadways, Coronation Road and Ashleigh Avenue, were commenced. The sum of £3,258 was spent on the Eastover Recreation Ground, and a splendid row of between 40 and 50 residences, facing the Recreation Ground and extending from St John Street to the exit leading to the riverside beyond the Infirmary, was regarded as another town improvement of a very attractive and substantial character.

The Mayor was Mr Henry William Pollard.

1906 At the General Election held on 26 January the result was as follows:

Mr H. G. Montgomery (Liberal)	4,422
Mr R. A. Saunders (Conservative)	4,405
(Liberal majority, 17)	

On 6 October the Co-operative Society premises in King Street were opened. They were demolished in 1981, and the site was used for building an extension of the Roman Catholic Church.

Continued prosperity in the town was evident from the number of new business enterprises that were opened, and the development of other businesses in various parts of the borough, including the extensive and handsome frontage of R. Squibbs & Son, and the furniture stores of Messrs. Bouchier in Eastover.

One of the most noteworthy improvements made during the year was the provision of a fire brigade station, scavengers' headquarters, and mortuary, at the rear of the Town Hall, which was formally opened by the Mayor, Alderman H. W. Pollard.

Emigration to Canada from Bridgwater and surrounding parishes continued on an extensive scale during the year.

A move was on foot for reducing the hours of hairdressers in the town. Most of the trade agreed to close at the following times–Monday and Tuesday 8.30 p.m.; Wednesday 9 p.m.; Thursday 2 p.m.; Friday 9 p.m.; Saturday 11 p.m.

An earthquake shock which occurred on Wednesday, 27 June was felt in Bridgwater at 9.45 a.m. In several factories, and especially at the Tone Vale Collar Factory, the sway of the earth was alarmingly experienced by the employees, and the machines moved in an ominous manner. In a number of households the peculiar motion of the earth created some consternation, but it could not be ascertained that any damage was done. The shock was felt all over South Wales and in many parts of the West of England. The disturbance was said to have lasted about three seconds.

On Thursday, 20 September, the official opening of the Bridgwater Public Library took place. The opening ceremony was performed by the Mayor, Mr H. W. Pollard, who had laid the foundation stone 11 months earlier. There was a great deal of speechmaking and a civic procession from the Council Chamber. A spacious marquee was erected in Blake Gardens, where the Mayor and Mayoress entertained the guests to refreshments. The Library was built at a cost of £3,500, provided through the generosity of Andrew Carnegie. The first Librarian was Mr Henry J. Croker who was appointed at a salary of £75 a year.

The Great Western Railway ran half-day excursions to London, leaving Bridgwater at 12.15 p.m., arriving at Paddington at 3.45 p.m. The train had a luncheon car serving hot or cold lunch for 2s., or teas 6d. and 1s. Return from Paddington at 12.55 p.m., with a supper car and hot supper (soup, joints, sweets, cheese and salad). The fare was 4s. 9d. return.

There were 53 fully licensed houses, 28 beer houses, and 14 other licenses in Bridgwater.

The population of the borough was 15,209.

Fine old Scotch whisky was 3s. 2d. a bottle, with an extra 4d. a bottle for very fine; brandy was 4s. a bottle, finest Jamaica rum was 3s. 2d., and gin 2s. 5d. from John L. Tripp, wine merchant, the *Royal Clarence* hotel. Men's suits from £2 2s. 0d., and overcoats from £1 0s. 0d. from C. H. Copp, Fore Street. Coal was 20s. a ton from Bryant & Son, Clare Street. J. Richards & Son, St Mary Street had Bridgwater sausages at 7d. a lb. 'I'll turn the mangle Pollie if you'll be mine' was the big advertisement of Squibbs & Son, furnishers, Eastover, for 'Easy, up-to-date wringing machines—the clothes come out as if they had been ironed'. Tobacco was from 3½d. to 5d. per ounce.

The Mayor was Mr Henry William Pollard.

1907 On 29 May the last vessel to be built and registered in Bridgwater was the *Irene,* a ketch of 99 tons, was launched.

Both in ancient and modern times worthy citizens were found who served two or more times in succession as chief magistrate and mayor of the town, but apparently no-one has beaten the record of Alderman H. W. Pollard, who enjoyed six years of office, in two sets of three, during the periods 1894-6 and 1905-7.

The terms of agreement for the employment of a farm worker provided for the payment of 12s. a week for a 70-hour week, plus 30s. for 'Harvest journeys' and the provision of one ton of coal, 100 faggots of wood, and a hogshead of cider. A quart of cider was also to be supplied free every day during harvest.

The Town Hall was packed with nearly a thousand people to hear speeches 'in favour of a better observance of the Sabbath'. The Mayor, Alderman H. W. Pollard, stated that the reason for the gathering was because the Sunday in England was becoming somewhat riotous. It was unanimously resolved to do all that could be done to discourage Sunday desecration.

Gentlemen's overcoats were £1 5s. 0d.; eggs 1s. 3d. a dozen; beef 6d. per lb. The excursion train return fare from Bridgwater to London was 5s. 6d.

Bridgwater celebrated Hospital Saturday in July in a big way with a large procession, fête and athletic sports. For many years the following Sunday was chosen for collections in all the churches and chapels; St Mary's Church was attended by the Mayor and Corporation. Hospital Saturday and Sunday were held every year and substantial sums were handed over to the funds of the Hospital.

1908 A large number of men found employment at the carriage sheds of the Great Western Railway, repairing rolling stock and making tarpaulin waggon covers. The town was a centre of the wicker-chair industry, making use of the withies which are grown plentifully in Sedgmoor and other low-lying lands near the junction of the Parrett and Tone. There were oil mills, where linseed and cotton seed cake was produced; engineering works, breweries, and cabinet works.

The women and girls of the town found employment in the large collar factories and in the steam laundry. In addition to the manufacturing industries a good trade was done both with the agricultural districts of which Bridgwater was the centre and with neighbouring towns.

On 29 July the new bandstand in Blake Gardens was opened by the Mayoress, Mrs Frank Wills. Bridgwater had been waiting 20 years for a site for this stand.

In the course of alterations to the house in Blake Street occupied by Mr W. H. Kitch, the birthplace of Admiral Robert Blake, drawings of ships and rigging, apparently of Elizabethan design were uncovered.

Thursday, 25 September, was the first day on which it was possible to make application for an old age pension, and in Bridgwater there was a surprising rush of applicants. Some people did not know their age!

The Bridgwater Branch of the National Farmer's Union was founded; it made rapid strides and now has a large membership.

The number of vessels entering the port was 1,730 of a total of 114,636 tons.

1909 The Head Post Office was transferred from High Street to the Cornhill.

Among books presented to the Free Library at Bridgwater in May was a copy of *The Great Revolt,* referring to the Bridgwater Riots of 1381.

In June members of the Bridgwater Rural District Council discussed an application from the Waterworks Inspector for an increase in salary. He was receiving 30s. a week. 'I think he is handsomely paid', said a member. The application was refused.

Speaking at the Bridgwater Quarter Sessions in April, the Recorder, Mr Wyndham Neave Slade, said it was a source of wonderment to him to note how extremely well-behaved the people of Bridgwater were. There were no cases to deal with.

For the first time in its history, Bridgwater Carnival took place on a Thursday, as apart from 5 November. Hitherto it had always been the custom to hold the Carnival on the 5th no matter on which day this fell, except for a Saturday or Sunday.

The provision of a footbridge over the River Parrett near Cranleigh Gardens was suggested, which would have been of great advantage to people wishing to get to the railway station.

In December a new building, known as the Bridgwater Roller Skating Rink, in Old Taunton Road, was opened. Roller-skating had 'caught on' in the town. The building included a refreshment room and tobacco stall.

The first old age pensions came into being worth 5s. a week to men and women aged 70 and over. In Bridgwater the number of people granted pensions was 233 out of 250 applicants. The pension was paid from 8 a.m. to 8 p.m. at the G.P.O., Cornhill, and at Eastover and North Street Post Offices.

The first taxicab to make its appearance in Bridgwater was on 16 October, due to the enterprise of Mr C. Carver the managing director of The Bridgwater Motor Co.

In November there was consternation in Bridgwater when it became known that the home of a local family had been 'raided' by the police in search for the makers of home-made fireworks. Widespread interest was occasioned by the subsequent prosecution. The court was told that the police found in the house quantities of gunpowder, partly-made and finished squibs, and a coffee-mill which had been used for grinding gunpowder. Despite all these disclosures the case was not pressed. Nevertheless, the magistrate imposed a fine of £10 and ordered confiscation of the squibs. Discussion ensued in the court room as to whether the squibs should be forfeited and sold, and the bench agreed to the order being made accordingly.

On 6 January Bridgwater was swept by a great snowstorm which gave the town a Russian appearance, which similarity was heightened by the appearance in the streets of a sleigh, drawn by two horses. The Mayor, Councillor R. O. Sully, asked that soup kitchens be opened in Westover and Eastover. The Stogursey carrier was unable to drive the van into Bridgwater as roads were almost impassable because of the blizzard.

In May a new building, 50ft. in height and comprising three storeys was erected for the Bridgwater Manufacturing Company at Monmouth Street. It provided accommodation for 200 additional hands.

J. H. Smyth-Piggott, the Agapemonite, was unfrocked at Wells.

The Bridgwater Corporation decided to suppress the sale of 'Teasers' at St Matthew's Fair. The majority of townspeople visiting the Fair agreed that the banning was sensible, and, although the fun was nothing like so fast and furious as in the past, exuberant youngsters found an excellent medium for letting off their excitement in the confetti. One of the reasons which activated the Town Council to stop the sale of 'Teasers' was the strong complaint made by the leading showmen. They said their business was interfered with by what they regarded as the abominable nuisance of 'teasering'.

The Mayor was Mr Richard Owen Sully.

1910 In February a gale raged at Bridgwater for three days, and extensive damage was caused to roofs, trees were uprooted on country roads, and flooding in fields assumed serious proportions.

The Eroder, the scouring-boat equipped with steam pumps to send powerful jets of water to disperse the silt, started shooting mud from the sides of the river at the Bridge.

At the General Election held on 20 January the result was as follows:

Mr R. A. Sanders (Conservative)	5,575
Mr H. Hicks (Liberal)	3,896

(Conservative majority, 1,679)

At the General Election held on 7 December, the result was as follows:

Mr R. A. Sanders (Conservative)	5,160
Mr. H. Hicks (Liberal)	3,779

(Conservative majority, 1,381)

On 3 February the Wicker Chair and Basket Works of Mr B. Saunders, Eastover, Bridgwater, was almost completely destroyed by fire. A large quantity of withies was saved, but many finished chairs were badly damaged, and the workmen lost most of their tools.

On 1 February, the first Labour Exchange opened in Bridgwater. The Exchange was a local Agency Office controlled by Mr Ennis in North Street.

In February, during a discussion on the proposed new police station at Northgate, a Town Councillor said one thing in favour of the site was that it was situated between the brewery and the workhouse.

On Friday, 16 December, a large portion of Bridgwater was visited by floods which did serious damage to property. It was reported that the flood came so suddenly that several residents were 'caught like rats in a trap'. Bridgwater was not the only place to suffer from the flooding on that occasion, for the gale on the previous day had whipped up the swollen waterways throughout the West Country and damage was widespread. It appears that shortly after six p.m. the Parrett showed signs of receding, then came an unexpected second bore. The tide broke over the banks, and in an incredibly short space of time the water flooded Salmon Parade to such a depth that the riverside railings were submerged. The flood rushed into Eastover, Barclay Street, Cranleigh Gardens, down to St John Street, and then into Devonshire Street and Wellington Road. The water was up to the axles of vehicles. At the other end of the town the streets were free from flooding, but the water managed to inundate basements in the Taunton Road, which is some distance from the river. Happily, the flood did not last very long, but it caused damage and not a little inconvenience.

The Mayor was Mr Henry William Pollard.

1911 On 4 January negotiations for the erection of a handsome new hall to be used by the Oddfellows in the town were completed for a site at West Quay, known as the *Anchor* inn. This old inn was a very popular hostelry for seafaring men.

On 12 April a meeting at Wembdon discussed a suggestion that a motor-bus service from the village to Bridgwater Station should be introduced, at a fare of 3d. all the way, or 1d. between the three fare stages.

Mr Hurford of the *Cottage* inn, Wembdon, while helping to extinguish a fire on some farm premises, fell from the roof and was killed almost instantaneously.

The population of the town was 16,757. On Monday, 4 April, the actual counting of the inhabitants took place.

In October, the Rev Dr Powell, who was the Vicar of St Mary's, Bridgwater, for about ten years, created a feeling of consternation by his unexpected announcement, made from the pulpit, that he had resigned the living and would shortly leave Bridgwater. The efforts made by the Church officials, leading members of the congregation, and others, including the selection of a deputation to wait upon the Bishop of the diocese, and the signing of a memorial by more than 3,000 inhabitants of the borough, with a view to the

Reverend gentleman's reinstatement, proved of no avail after the resignation had been accepted at headquarters.

The formation of a Morganians' Association in Bridgwater this year was welcomed by both the old and the new boys associated with the famous school bearing the founder's name. The School was well attended under the leadership of the Rev W. E. Catlow.

After 1973 Dr Morgan's School ceased to exist and it was incorporated along with the Girls' Grammar School into Haygrove School, which is a Comprehensive School for pupils aged from eleven to sixteen.

On 11 March it was stated that only one vessel was lying in the river at Bridgwater between Town Bridge and the mouth of the Parrett; such an absence of craft in the river could not be recalled.

In May, owing to the efforts of the Bridgwater Trader's Association all the tailors, outfitters, drapers and milliners decided to close their businesses in future at one p.m. on Thursdays.

On Saturday, 17 June, Mr W. H. Roberts, of New Road, Bridgwater, died. Mr Roberts was well known as the head of the West of England Carriage Works. When the two-wheeled cycle was introduced from the Continent, his firm were the pioneers of the industry. It was an industry which, in the opinion of many, Bridgwater should have retained.

On 21 June a barge laden with 11,000 bricks, both the property of Colthurst, Symons & Co., Ltd., sank in the River Parrett near the Bridgwater Gas Works.

In June, at the Town Hall, the employees of the Tone Vale Manufacturing Company assembled to see a presentation made to the principals of the Company, Messrs. H. J. Van Trump and W. H. J. Masding.

Thursday, 28 June, was a memorable day with the town in Coronation dress. A fête and gala were held at Taunton Road football ground, where a pushball game took place. Crowds of people went to the top of Wembdon Hill to see the Coronation bonfires, 31 of which were visible. There was no attempt at boisterous rejoicing, and the assembly was of a quiet and staid order.

In March the Property Committee of the Town Council reported having received 15 tenders for the erection of the new Court House and police station in Northgate and on their recommendation the tender of Mr J. E. Fursland of Bridgwater amounting to the sum of £7,350 was accepted. The stone was laid by the Mayor, Mr H. W. Pollard. The police station was opened in January 1913.

The Monmouth Street Methodist Church was opened in April by Mrs R. A. Sanders and Mr Joseph Butler of Bristol. The site cost £1,338 and the Church cost £3,000; it has seating for 430 persons.

1912 The *Bijou* theatre in St Mary Street was opened in November and a crowded and enthusiastic audience attended the first performance.

A large number of people emigrated to Australia and Canada.

A man in the employ of the Bridgwater Hauling Company was summoned for driving a steam-propelled engine at a speed of more than two miles an hour. He was fined in his absence 10s and costs.

The newly-established golf ball factory in Friarn Street proved a very successful venture.

The number of ships entering the port of Bridgwater was 1,586 of a total of 105,972 tons.

The new Masonic Temple in King Square was opened with an imposing ceremony and was a noteworthy addition to the town's institutions.

The much esteemed Headmaster of Dr Morgan's School, the Rev W. E. Catlow, had the gratification of reporting not only that the school was 'absolutely full and its accommodation taxed to the utmost' but that 'out of 34 candidates presented at the last examination as many as 31 passed, 17 being placed in the honours division'.

In July a strike in the collar-making trade which started at Taunton extended to Bridgwater, where there were 1,000 hands idle. The firms affected were the Tone Vale Manufacturing Company (of which Mr H. J. Van Trump and Mr W. H. J. Masding were the principals) and Mr Moody's factories in New Road and Dampiet Street. There was a lively parade of the workers through the streets of the town to the Eastover Recreation Ground.

A huge whale was washed up on the shore at Stolford, near Bridgwater. It was described as a fine specimen of the bottle-nosed whale. It was first discovered when it was about half a mile from the shore, spouting water. The whale had apparently got into shallow water and lashed itself about on the mud until it died. It was 19ft. in length and weighed about four tons. Hundreds of people journeyed from Bridgwater and district to view the carcass. The whale was so large that it had to be cut into four sections and buried.

The Mayor was Mr Richard Owen Sully.

1913 A doctor complained at a Bridgwater inquest that at the borough mortuary there was no hot water, no towels, and not even any soap. Also, he himself had had to go to the police station for keys to the building.

The last sitting of the Borough Magistrates at the Town Hall, High Street, was on Monday, 27 January, the day prior to the official opening of the new police station at Northgate. The first case was heard on 1 February, when the defendant who appeared on a charge of being drunk and disorderly was told by the bench that although it was felt to be a very serious case, as it was the first one it would be discharged.

Mr Henry Laver of West Quay, Bridgwater, caught a porpoise weighing 168lb. It was believed to be the largest sea-hog ever captured in the River Parrett.

A good deal of excitement was aroused a day or two before the famous Guy Fawkes Carnival in Bridgwater, by the threatened intervention of the Home Office authorities who, it was announced, had communicated with the Chief Constable on the subject with a view to the prevention of the discharge of fireworks in the main thoroughfare and the ignition of the customary bonfire on the Cornhill. The Carnival Committee expressed their determination to celebrate the Carnival in the usual way and the Chief Constable, acting presumably on the advice of the Watch Committee, very wisely refrained from active interference. The announcement of this intention not to interfere on the eve of the demonstration allayed the excitement and probably averted proceedings of a riotous character, and the whole affair proved as harmless and satisfactory as in former years.

The Shops Act came into force in Bridgwater with regard to the trades carried on by outfitters, hosiers, hatters, drapers, milliners, tailors and boot- and shoe-makers and dealers. In future the shops devoted to these businesses were to close at 7 p.m. on Monday, Tuesday and Wednesday, at 1 p.m. on Thursday, 8.30 p.m. on Friday, and at 10 p.m. on Saturday.

The Mayoress of Bridgwater, in the company of the Mayor and the Borough Surveyor, planted two chestnut trees in the Eastover Recreation ground. It was intended to form an avenue of trees the whole length of the Recreation ground.

Most noteworthy and of the greatest importance was the determination that had been arrived at to form a conciliation Board for Bridgwater and district, with a view to the amicable settlement of labour disputes, which unhappily had been so prevalent lately. With regard to labour unrest and temporary suspension of work during the past year at the brickyards and factories where female labour was largely used, it was confidently anticipated that hereafter any renewal of such differences between employers and employees would be peaceably adjusted without resorting to strikes, which entailed so much mischief to the whole of the country.

The engine which opened and closed the G.W.R. telescopic bridge spanning the River Parrett broke down. The bridge was across the river at the time and as it was nearly high water, it was imperative that the bridge should be withdrawn. Gangers eventually pulled back the bridge by means of ropes and chains.

The new Territorial Hall in New Road, Eastover was built and was officially opened in May; among distinguished visitors attending was the Marquis of Bath.

An application by a North Petherton licensee for an extension of licensed hours until 4 a.m. for a peapickers' supper and dance was refused. The Bench considered midnight quite late enough.

It was interesting to note that in September Bridgwater people had the opportunity of witnessing aeroplane flights arranged by Mr H. Carver and Mr B. C. Hicks, who had already given exhibitions of the art of flying at Weston and Burnham.

Bridgwater Town Council first voted its Mayor a salary of £125 a year.

January saw the formal opening of the new Court House and police station in Northgate, Bridgwater. It was an event of considerable local importance, and although the new structure proved more costly than was at first anticipated and a large proportion of the ratepayers would have been much more satisfied if a better site had been selected, it constituted a great public improvement which was badly needed.

A record sum of £220 was raised by Bridgwater Amateur Dramatic Society's production of 'Merrie England'.

On 3 September a well-attended open-air mass meeting was held at East Quay in connection with a strike of workers at Messrs Barham Bros, over a refusal to increase wages.

The Mayor was Mr David Bradfield.

1914 On 18 March a violent gale swept over Bridgwater and district, and did a great deal of damage. Branches were torn from trees, chimney pots came down, and the river burst its banks in many places. Roofing at the motor garage of Thos. Hamlin & Co., in Monmouth Street, was blown down.

On 29 April an outbreak of fire occurred in the early hours of Sunday morning at the Bath Bridge Engineering Works. The premises, which were very extensive, were owned by Messrs E. Millard & Son. Damage was estimated at £700.

On 8 April schemes for a new length of road from the foot of Wembdon Hill to the entrance of Cockerhurst Farm, and to widen the existing road to Wembdon Hill, were passed by Bridgwater Rural District Council. Mr T. M. Reed, clerk, said that the cost of the new road would be £1,888 2s. 8d.

On 15 April a very interesting addition was made to St Mary's Church by the erection over the Vicar's stall in the Chancel of a neatly-designed panel containing a list of all the vicars of Bridgwater, from the year 1170.

A new telephone call office was available to the public at the Bridgwater Post Office.

The suggestion that, because of the war, a temporary hospital should be set up at Bridgwater was discussed at a meeting held in the Council Chamber. The proposed hospital would be at the Skating Rink and Club, Taunton Road.

Considerable damage was done when fire broke out at premises in King Street, occupied by Mr Gill, who carried on the business of blouse manufacturer.

On 3 June workers at the West of England Cabinet and Perambulator Works were threatening to strike over the rate of wages, hours and working conditions. Workmen refused to listen to their employers, who in public announcements said that if a strike occurred they would close their works permanently.

On 6 May Mr Harry Van Trump, a member of the firm of the Tone Vale Manufacturing Co., Bridgwater, had a narrow escape from drowning. Mr Van Trump was a passenger in an aeroplane piloted by Mr Salmet, which was being flown from Minehead to Weston. About a mile off the shore of Watchet, the engines stopped, and the plane plunged into the water. A lifeboat was launched and the two men were picked up unhurt.

At a meeting of the Somerset Agricultural Instruction Committee at Bridgwater, Mr Neville Grenville moved that at future meetings the Press should be excluded, on the grounds that the presence of reporters encouraged people to make unnecessary speeches and discouraged those who wanted to do business. As no other member favoured the motion, Mr Grenville withdrew it.

King Square 'hit the headlines' when Britain was in the throes of suffragette activities. In June a young woman arrived in Bridgwater from London and 'took rooms' in King Square which was then a residential area, in which the houses were occupied by many of the more wealthy townspeople. The arrival of a stranger in their midst became a topic of conversation and as it was suspected that the young woman was connected with the suffragette movement, the police were informed, and officers, including the late Inspector Storey, kept watch on the house. Suffragettes had a habit of setting fire to houses and concealing bombs in churches and other buildings. Police activity in Bridgwater reached fever point on a Sunday morning when the stranger entered St Mary's Church carrying a 'Dorothy' bag. She entered the building with Inspector Storey hot on her heels. He took up a seat in the pew immediately behind her. Of course, everyone in Bridgwater knew Inspector Storey and they sensed that something was afoot. The young woman clutched her 'Dorothy' bag and almost simultaneously there was a loud bang! The noise, however, was not that of an exploding bomb, but of a door being slammed in another part of the Church. The service ended, the stranger left the church—again hotly pursued by Inspector Storey and another policeman. They kept the woman in view until she reached Bower Lane on the Bath Road when, as a *Mercury* report of the incident stated 'It was not deemed necessary to follow her further'. Was she really a suffragette? No-one will ever know.

Indication of the impact the war was having on the town: the Albion Rugby Football Club's annual meeting had been postponed; people were flocking to the Goathurst Road, North Petherton, to see the searchlights in the Bristol Channel; the Territorial Camp on Salisbury Plain had disbanded; and the Infantry from Bridgwater sent to Devonport for garrison duty.

The 'C' (Bridgwater) Squadron of the West Somerset Yeomanry under Major Stenhouse was mobilised, and men and their horses were billeted in various licensed houses in the town.

The Chief Constable (Mr W. J. Davey) received orders from the War Office to prepare horses and waggons for military purposes. They were taken to Aplin & Son's yard, George Street, or to the yard at the *Malt Shovel* hotel. Over 150 horses had been bought.

A big and sudden jump in food prices led to a resolution at an open-air Labour meeting calling on the Government to take complete control of supplies to secure that the poor were not exploited by unpatriotic merchants. Mr S. J. Plummer was the main speaker, but Mr Ernest Bevin, of Bristol, also gave a rousing address.

Many men attached to the Bridgwater and district postal staff were among the Reservists called up, and from the Borough Police Force P.C. Fry had to report to Newcastle. The only foreign vessel at the Docks was a Swedish craft and there were instructions to keep her and the crew at Bridgwater for the time being.

The G.W.R. bridge was guarded night and day.

Bridgwater Rugby Club abandoned all matches arranged for September.

By the last week in August there had been a public meeting in the Council Chamber to discuss the equipment of a temporary hospital for the wounded, and a great recruitment meeting addressed by Major Archer Shee and Colonel Trevor, and the enrolment of a large number of special constables.

The Mayor was Mr David Bradfield, who died in office, followed by Mr Francis George Haggett.

1915 The 10 March was a happy day for many employees in Bridgwater who received rises in their wages. Those working in the brickyards of the town had received a general rise of one shilling per week, and the Bridgwater Wicker Works Ltd., now Squibbs Ltd., advanced the wages of their hands for the second time in a few weeks.

At a meeting of the Bridgwater Rural District Council it was decided to raise the wages of all Council workmen to one level—17s. 6d. per week.

In July a serious fire, involving damage of over £1,000 occurred when the extensive premises of Messrs G. Randle & Son, timber merchants and sawyers, were partially destroyed.

The Mayor was Mr Francis George Haggett.

1916 On 8 March the *Palace* theatre, Penel Orlieu, was opened by Alderman F. Wills; it was capable of seating 800 persons.

It was decided to insure St Mary's Parish Church for £23,500 against damage by enemy aircraft.

The General Post Office was open from 7 a.m. to 9 p.m., and on Sundays from 8.30 a.m. to 10 a.m.

In a collision on the river just below Chilton brickyard, the steamship *Devon,* owned by Peace, Ltd., collided with the steamship *A.1* belonging to Hunt & Co. Both were badly damaged.

The Mayor was Mr Francis George Haggett.

1917 In June serious damage was occasioned to crops by a great storm which visited Bridgwater and district; lands and roadways were badly flooded, as were several houses in Hamp Ward to a depth of several feet.

A new wicker works industry was started at the Chilton Street Mills by Mr S. C. F. Clark of Plymouth, and many employees found profitable employment.

One of the longest frosts and coldest winters for many years ended in mid-February. The River Parrett had an almost arctic appearance, and navigation was blocked for a fortnight and the canal was frozen over.

The Mayor was Mr Francis George Haggett.

1918 An extensive jam factory was established at Wembdon which was considerably extended in 1919.

In Bridgwater it was a source of infinite pride and gratification to the inhabitants that they could justly claim to have contributed their full share of participation in the war that terminated this year. First and foremost the melancholy fact was recorded that the 'Roll of Honour' has shown that as many as 308 men belonging to the borough had fallen in action, and it was hoped that shortly a movement to perpetuate their memory with a fitting and lasting public memorial would get underway.

At the General Election held in December, the result was as follows:

Lieut.-Colonel R. A. Sanders (Conservative)	12,587
Mr S. J. Plummer (Labour)	5,771

(Conservative majority, 6,816)

In June there was no contest at the by-election in the Bridgwater Division, and Lieut.-Colonel R. A. Sanders (Conservative) was returned unopposed.

An influenza epidemic was rampant in the town, and doctors were so overworked that cases had to be put on the waiting list. Schools remained closed.

The Mayor was Mr Francis George Haggett.

1919 In August a sensation was caused in the town, by a daring robbery at a jeweller's shop in St Mary Street. A huge stone was hurled through a plate-glass window in the early hours of the morning and £50 worth of goods were stolen. The perpetrator of the outrage remained undiscovered.

The Bridgwater Young Men's Association acquired new premises in Castle Street, and was then known as the Castle Club. They were far better and more commodious than those in St Mary Street. A splendid billiards room was provided.

The 'Victory Loan' Week in July was attended with gratifying results; a total of £100,000 was the quota expected for Bridgwater, but the amount actually raised was no less than £162,327. In recognition of this remarkable success the town was presented with a tank in October, which at a ceremony was placed on a site in St John Street in close proximity to the Great Western Railway Station. Another war trophy, consisting of a gun, was offered to the town and accepted.

The Mayor was Mr Samuel Berry.

1920 In February the club premises of the 'Comrades of the Great War' in St Mary Street were opened and the organisation proved a very successful one.

In March a strike of 200 employees of the Bridgwater Manufacturing Company took place and did not collapse until several weeks had passed. The employees returned to work on condition that there would be no victimisation.

The Mayor was Mr Samuel Berry.

1921 The population of Bridgwater was 15,962.

The first meeting of the Bridgwater Chamber of Commerce was held in April. A Council representative of the various industries in the town was appointed. Mr Edwin Brown proposed that the attention of the Council be directed to the present service of passenger trains on the Great Western Railway and the Somerset and Dorset Railway, with a view to obtaining improved facilities for Bridgwater.

The Mayor was Mr Samuel Berry.

1922 Quantock Road, Bridgwater, was opened.

On 25 October the employment exchange was moved from the old police station, High Street, to premises at 14 King Square.

An amusing incident occurred at the election when Sir Robert Sanders (Conservative) defeated Alderman W. E. Morse (Liberal). The election was in progress and a steeplejack who was removing the weathercock from the spire of St Mary's Church for regilding had placed a red flag on the spire; this caused an outcry and the man was forced to remove it.

A Cockney steeplejack visited the Vicar and asked if he might climb the steeple and ascertain whether any repairs were necessary. The story goes that this was agreed to, and the man brought down some crumbling masonry to show that his services were needed. The work was entrusted to him and all went well until the morning of polling day. Then attached to the weathervane was hoisted a red flag. The steeplejack admitted that he was responsible, and added proudly, 'I'm a Red'. Told by the Vicar to go up and take if down at once, he replied, 'I shall do nothing of the sort, if you want it down, then go up and fetch it'.

At the General Election held on 16 November the result was as follows:

Sir R. A. Sanders (Conservative)	11,240
Alderman W. E. Morse (Liberal)	11,121
Lieut-Col. Beauchamp Williams (Labour)	1,598

(Conservative majority, 119)

In this year the Bridgwater Carnival was filmed and this aroused great interest.

The Mayor was Mr Frederick H. Allen.

1923 At the General Election held in December, the result was as follows:

Mr W. E. Morse (Liberal)	13,778
Rt Hon Sir R. A. Sanders (Conservative)	12,347

(Liberal majority, 1,431)

Derby Day when Steve Donoghue won on Papyrus was a memorable occasion. During the lunch hour there was a betting raid on a public house in the centre of the town when several of the customers were locked up for the night.

Considerable activity along the coast near Kilve raised hopes of a huge industry coming to the district, as rich oil shale had been discovered with prospects of huge supplies of oil. Unfortunately nothing came of the venture.

The Mayor was Mr W. H. J. Masding.

1924 At the General Election held on 29 October, the result was as follows:

Mr B. Crompton-Wood (Conservative)	14,283
Mr W. E. Morse (Liberal)	10,842
Mr J. M. Boltz (Labour)	1,966

(Conservative majority, 3,441)

Blake House, Blake Street, was purchased by the town as the Admiral Blake Museum. The house had suffered many 'restorations' in the past.

The town's memorial to those who fell in the Great War was erected in King Street and was unveiled by the Earl of Cavan.

This year saw the last of the Cornhill Carnival bonfires. The bonfire was banned because of a new road surface.

The Rev W. E. Catlow, M.A., retired after 24 years as Headmaster of Dr Morgan's School. His valuable services, both to the School and to many departments of public and church life, will be long remembered.

A public enquiry was held at the Town Hall in July when an application for an order to construct a light railway from Bridgwater to Watchet was considered at an estimated cost of £237,000. Nothing more, however, was heard of it.

The Mayor was Mr H. M. B. Ker.

1925 The Bridgwater Cricket Club had a very successful season, during which a handsome new pavilion was opened at the Parks.

The number of unemployed registered at Christmas at the Bridgwater Labour Exchange was 525, made up of 418 men, 71 women, 19 boys, and 17 girls. This was a substantial decrease compared with the Christmas week of 1924 when the total was 664, of whom 491 were men, 128 women, 24 boys, and 21 girls.

The November Carnival was held without a bonfire on the Cornhill this year, but the absence of that familiar feature in no way detracted from the success of the annual saturnalia.

A site was secured off the Quantock Road for a new cemetery for the western site of the town.

A 'Beam' wireless station was established at Huntworth to receive messages from Canada and South Africa.

In addition to two cinemas, a theatre was held at the Town Hall, and the old *Empire* theatre in St Mary Street was reopened.

The main thoroughfares of the town were remade with a beautiful smooth surface that was the delight of motorists, but the terror of horse owners.

A great advance was made at the Hospital by the provision of a splendidly-arranged children's ward and of wireless instruments for the patients.

The Mayor was Mr Walter Deacon.

1926 The Admiral Blake Museum, Blake Street, was opened to the public on 16 April.

This year in order to stimulate public interest in a proposed town pageant, a most original idea was put forward. The 26 June, it was announced, would be 'Charter Day'. In actual fact the first of our royal charters was sealed on 26 June in the year 1200, so this was a simple anniversary.

A ceremony took place on the Cornhill on 26 June and immense crowds gathered to see the impressive civic pageantry and to hear the words of the ancient charter read out. The B.B.C. broadcast the proceedings and they were widely reported in the national press. The idea had proved a tremendous success and preparations for the town pageant went forward with the support of the whole population of the town.

This year a new feature was the revival of the Bridgwater Races in July, after a lapse of many years. The races were successfully held at Durleigh.

The Bridgwater and District Canine Society was formed after the fine show of dogs on Easter Monday.

The Mayor was Mr Walter Deacon.

1927 The Bridgwater pageant was produced in June of this year. The whole of the pageant was finely presented and organised splendidly and with much thoroughness, and the display bore comparison with great pageants in the past. Its appeal was very strong as the town and district was of great importance at times in England's history. The pageant was presented in delightful surroundings, at Sydenham Manor historic estate near Bridgwater. There were nearly 1,000 performers in costume of varying periods. The chief scenes were of Admiral Blake and Sedgmoor, though other episodes dealt with the visits of King John, who gave the town its charter; with the Bridgwater Riots in 1381; with the funeral of Sir Hugh Luttrell; with St Matthew's Fair in 1588; and, finally, with an 18th-century hustings scene. The Mayor, Alderman Walter Deacon, was the leading spirit in the enterprise.

The town experienced a terrific thunderstorm in July, and several parts were flooded.

Navigation near the Docks in the River Parrett was blocked for a while in the summer when a foreign steamer, the *Masuren,* with a large cargo of timber, capsized.

The town was still faced with the serious problem of unemployment because of which the business of the town suffered.

1928 By the Bridgwater Corporation Act, the Borough and Parish of Bridgwater was extended so as to include part of the Parish of Bridgwater Without.

On 21 March the foundation stone of Quantock Road Cemetery was laid by Alderman W. Deacon. The cemetery is about fourteen acres in extent and has a chapel with 56 seats.

The Town Council passed a scheme to lay out Victoria Park at a cost of £2,050.

The Mayor was Mr Frederick Oswald Symons.

1929 The Bridgwater Dog Show was held on Whit Monday and was a gratifying success. The Bridgwater Races were held in this year, but received poor support and so it was decided that they should be discontinued.

The Bridgwater Town Council decided to give their workmen a week's holiday with pay.

On 26 November, the *Arcade* cinema, Eastover, was opened.

An occurrence which was almost unique was that the electors chose Mr H. J. Squibbs and his two sons as their representatives on the Town Council.

The result of the General Election held 31 May was as follows:

Mr R. P. Croom-Johnson (Conservative)	15,440
Mr J. W. Molden (Liberal)	11,161
Mr J. M. Boltz (Labour)	6,423

(Conservative majority, 4,279)

It was decided by the Somerset Educational Committee to take over Dr Morgan's School, and to erect a new school in Durleigh on a site of about eleven acres.

The Mayor was Mr Frederick Oswald Symons.

1930 In January, Bridgwater was visited by a great gale, which did considerable damage, the most serious of which was the complete demolition of the cabinet works of Messrs Gillson Bros, on the Bristol Road.

This was not a particularly bright year for the trades and industries of the town, which had shared with other parts of the country the serious depression, and the number of unemployed showed little signs of abatement. One encouraging development was the erection of a new factory at Chilton for the mass production of bricks and tiles which, it was hoped, would increase the local output of these commodities.

The most tragic event was the sad although heroic death of the Vicar of Bridgwater, the Rev Seymour Berry, who was drowned whilst attempting to save his little daughter when bathing at Hayle in Cornwall. The funeral was one of the largest seen in the town for many years, and was a striking tribute to the high esteem in which Mr Berry was held.

The Mayor was Mr Frederick Oswald Symons.

1931 At the General Election held on 27 October, the result was as follows:

Mr R. P. Croom-Johnson (Conservative)	24,041
Mr J. M. Boltz (Labour)	3,974

(Conservative majority, 17,067)

The Victoria Road Bridge was opened by the Mayor, Mr Frederick Oswald Symons.

The population of Bridgwater was 17,139.

1932 The opening of the new golf course at Enmore was an event of great interest. The course proved most popular and the Club enjoyed a large and increasing membership. The opening ceremony was performed by Mr R. P. Croom-Johnson, K.C., M.P.

This year was a period associated with a good deal of trade depression, and the unemployment situation became acute. The total unemployed was 1,847 in December as against 1,250 at the same period previously.

The Mayor was Mr Charles Bryer.

1933 In January Bridgwater had a peak figure of 2,100 unemployed, over 31 per cent. of the insured population.

In the Somerset Review Order, the Borough and Parish of Bridgwater was extended to include part of the Parish of Bridgwater Without and Wembdon.

The 10 June was the last day on which Bridgwater's other weekly newspaper, *The Independent,* was printed. It was announced that *The Bridgwater Mercury* had purchased the copyright.

It was almost a record year for dry weather with a glorious summer, though, fortunately, the town had not suffered the experience of other parts of the country where the water shortage had become so acute that supplies had to be seriously rationed.

The principal event of the year was the holding in the summer of a 'Bridgwater Week'. Various items of an attractive programme, such as a shopping carnival, a fête, a gala at the swimming baths, and various events in the Blake Gardens, drew large crowds of people.

A Bridgwater Rotary Club was established with the Mayor, Mr Charles Bryer as President. Weekly luncheons with short addresses commenced at the inauguration of the Club on 4 December.

During the year the Town Council acquired a new fire engine which was acknowledged to be a great acquisition to the town's services.

1934 On Sunday, 4 June, Bridgwater witnessed one of the biggest fires for many years at Hickman's, in Eastover, and at the adjoining *White Hart* hotel. The fire raged close to the hospital buildings and nurses took part in the fire-fighting.

An ox was roasted at Penel Orlieu, Bridgwater, in aid of hospital extensions.

Whilst carrying out excavations in preparation for building a new council house estate, some workmen discovered part of the Friary buildings. The bases of several pillars were uncovered. They probably stood in the Infirmary. Unfortunately the site was filled in again and it now lies beneath the council house estate in Friarn Avenue. The only relics that can be seen consist of masonry and some interesting paving tiles which are displayed in the Museum.

An event of importance to shoppers in Bridgwater was the opening on Friday, 2 March, of Marks & Spencer's store on the Cornhill.

In March, an application by Bridgwater licensees for a summertime extension of hours until 10.30 p.m. was opposed by clergymen and temperence women and the application was refused.

Shopping was very much cheaper: shirts were from 4s. 11d.; suits to measure 37s. 6d.; men's slippers 1s. 11½d.; smart overcoats 17s. 6d.; ladies' fur-trimmed coats 21s.; and umbrellas 1s. 11d. Port and sherry from 3s. per bottle; champagne from 6s. 6d. per bottle; Scotch and Irish whisky from 11s. 6d. per bottle; finest Australian wines, full strength, red or white, 2s. 9d. per bottle.

Thursday, 11 May was a day of great importance in the history of Bridgwater Hospital, for it saw the opening of the new wing and an x-ray department, provided at a cost of £11,000.

On Friday, 23 June, Sir Edward Hilton Young, after formally opening the new reservoir and extension of the waterworks at Ashford, was made first Freeman of the Borough.

On Monday, 26 June, Bridgwater experienced a thunderstorm of great severity. It began at 4 p.m. and in an hour had flooded many streets. Gutters and drains could not cope with the amount of water after the prolonged drought.

The Mayor was Mr Frederick John Reed.

1935 The new Cattle Market was opened in Bath Road and the 26 June was the last day that cattle were sold in the Old Market at Penel Orlieu.

When the new Cattle Market was opened, allegations were made in a letter to the Council by the Committee of the Bridgwater Women's Total Abstinence Association of scenes which were a 'disgrace to the town', following the issue of free drinks at the opening ceremony. It was stated that intoxicated women returned home too late to get their husbands' dinners after they had been drinking at the town's expense; and that women had carried away alcoholic drinks in jugs and bottles. The Town Clerk said he had replied to the letter and that it was a most scurrilous attack on the people of Bridgwater. He contended that the town spent less in hospitality than any other of its size in England. One councillor said there was intense feeling in the town on the question, and another remarked, 'It is just as well for them to have a free beer as for you to have free whisky when you opened your waterworks'.

One of the most serious fires in memory occurred at Messrs Bouchier's furniture stores in St Mary Street in September.

At the General Election held on 14 November the result was as follows:

Mr R. P. Croom-Johnson (Conservative)	17,939
Mr N. D. Blake (Liberal)	7,370
Mr A. W. Loveys (Labour)	6,240

(Conservative majority, 10,569)

The British Cellophane Co., Ltd., began building a large factory on a site which was part of the ancient manor of Sydenham. The local authorities encouraged the establishment of new industry in the town which was in a rather depressed state, especially the brick and tile trade.

The Mayor was Mr Frederick John Reed.

1936 On 13 July the *Odeon* theatre was opened by Mr R. P. Croom-Johnson, K.C., M.P. The Mayor, Mr F. J. Reed, attended the ceremony with other well-known people, including Lord St Audries. The builders of the theatre were Messrs H. W. Pollard & Sons, of Bridgwater. It has seating capacity of 1,600.

Exciting scenes were witnessed at Bridgwater on the evening of Thursday, 10 January, during the height of a gale. The River Parrett overflowed its banks and water extended for a considerable distance into St John Street.

On 24 June a severe thunderstorm, following a day of great heat and sunshine, caused flooding and damage in parts of West Somerset. In Bridgwater both North Street and Taunton Road were flooded, and a house was struck by lightning at Highbridge.

In March, lack of public support was blamed for the closing down of Bridgwater Amateur Operatic Society, which made its first public appearance in 1909.

1937 There was severe flooding in the North Street area of the town on St Swithin's Day, and the force of flood water caused the collapse of the canal bridge wall in Wembdon Road. Nearly five inches of rain fell in the one day. The total rainfall on St Swithin's Day, 1937, was two and three-quarters inches.

However, on the previous day (14 July) two and a quarter inches of rain fell. This could have been all in one storm with two and a quarter inches falling before midnight on 14 July, hence it is true to say that 'nearly five inches of rain fell in one day'.

The new Wembdon Road School was first opened for pupils. It was described as a new 'wonder' school. Mr A. Wevell (Headmaster) and Miss Sawtell (Headmistress) were in charge.

It was said that Bridgwater might well be proud of the new Dr Morgan's School in Durleigh Road. The building was stated to be almost the last word in secondary schools.

On 17 October the Bridgwater Rural District Council met for the first time in their new offices at the Priory, St Mary Street. The Chairman was the Rev P. T. Pryce-Mitchell; the Clerk, Mr H. G. Blay; and the Surveyor, Mr L. S. Clatworthy.

The spire, tower and outside of St Mary's Church were examined and repaired. The inside walls and roof were cleaned and washed, and the west end wall replastered. The sanctuary was remodelled and an oak communion rail put in place of the brass one. The weathercock was taken down and re-gilded. The entire work cost £2,650. The renovation scheme was inaugurated to mark the anniversary of the building of the spire in 1367 and a commemoration of the 4th centenary of the translation of the Bible into the English language. The scheme was completed in June 1938.

The Mayor was Mr William Chard.

1938 On 11 June it was stated at a meeting of the District Employment Committee that there were 1,343 people registered as unemployed in the town in May compared with 981 a year ago.

The highest honour the profession of pharmacy can offer was conferred on Mr Walter Deacon of Bridgwater, in London, when he was elected President of the Pharmaceutical Society of Great Britain.

Mr Reginald Croom-Johnson, M.P. for Bridgwater, was appointed a judge of the King's Bench Division.

In July the new reservoir at Durleigh was filled with water. It had been constructed to meet the demands of new industry and it was intended to ensure an adequate supply of water for a long time ahead.

At the By-Election held on 17 November, the result was as follows:

Mr Vernon Bartlett (Independent)	19,540
Mr R. G. Heathcote-Amory (Conservative)	17,208

(Independent majority, 2,332)

This By-Election was a very important one and aroused tremendous interest. The declaration was two hours later than expected, and a heavy poll of 82.4 per cent. was believed to be a record for a by-election.

Rich oil beds near Bridgwater came prominently in the news. It was stated that experiments along the west Somerset coast had renewed belief that the area was rich in oil shale. However, after exhaustive tests and experiments nothing came of the venture.

Alderman Samuel Berry, a native of Bridgwater, was honoured by being presented with the Freedom of the Borough, on 1 July. He had served over 40 years on the Council and figured largely in the public life of the Borough.

After a three-days hearing a Select Committee of the House of Commons declared in favour of Bridgwater Rural District Council who had opposed Bridgwater Corporation's move to include the Parish of Wembdon as part of the Borough.

After a lapse of many years, the ringers of St Mary's Church held a supper at the *Mansion House* inn.

By the Ministry of Health Provisional Order Confirmation (Bridgwater Extension) Act 1938, the Borough of Bridgwater was extended by the addition of part of the Parish of Bridgwater Without.

During the early hours of one morning the Blake Statue on the Cornhill was disfigured when a mixture of whiting was thrown or plastered over it.

The offer of the owner to donate the site of Westonzoyland with a memorial erected to commemorate the Battle of Sedgemoor to the Town Council aroused considerable interest.

The annual report on the trade of the town and port, which was presented to the 28th annual meeting of the Bridgwater Incorporated Chamber of Commerce, Shipping and Agriculture, showed that during 1938 a total of 797 vessels entered the port, compared with 828 the previous year. Import tonnage showed a decrease of 3,126 on 1937.

The Mayor was Mr James Boltz, followed by Mr Louis H. Palmer.

1939 Bridgwater Fire Brigade was made the victim of a silly hoax. A telephone call was received at the station to go to a fire at the Somerset Farm Institute, Cannington. When they arrived there was no sign of a fire. Efforts were made to trace the call, but without success.

Workmen unearthed a number of human bones while reconstructing premises in Clare Street, at the back of the offices of the Bridgwater Gas Light Company in High Street.

Alderman F. J. Reed moved a resolution calling on the Town Council to pass a standing order making unseemly behaviour or the use of bad language in the Council Chamber an offence to be dealt with by the Council. The resolution was lost.

At the annual meeting of the Bridgwater and District Nursing Association and Mary Stanley Home it was reported that premises at Castle Street had been acquired which would enable the staff to be given more adequate accommodation and would also provide eight additional maternity beds, making 25 in all.

England's oldest lady, Mrs Emma Coate, died at North Curry, aged one hundred and eight. She had lived through six reigns.

Thousands of evacuees, mostly London children, arrived at the Great Western Station at the beginning of September.

Messrs S. Leffman, Ltd., brassière manufacturers, opened a factory at Bridgwater towards the end of September. It was situated at Washington Gardens, for many years the workshops of Mr T. Stockham, builder and contractor.

The Bishop of Clifton (Mgr Lee) opened the Missionary Convent of the Holy Rosary at 'Eastcroft', Durleigh Road.

Bridgwater Town Council agreed to make an appeal through the County Council to the Ministry of Transport to proceed immediately with the proposed new by-pass for Bridgwater.

The Bath and West of England Agricultural Show was held at Huntworth Park, Bridgwater, from Wednesday, 24 May, to Saturday, 27 May. The Show was a great success. It was favoured with beautiful hot, sunny weather. The total attendance was 55,623. The Town Council spent about £100 on street decorations. The Duke of Somerset was President of the Society and the Show was opened by the Mayor, Mr Louis Palmer.

The old year was tolled out as usual, and the new one ushered in with merry peals on the bells of St Mary's Church. A large crowd of merrymakers assembled on the Cornhill and joined in singing Auld Lang Syne, and there were blasts from hooters and the discharge of fireworks to welcome 1940.

1940 In January a vote was taken at the Bridgwater Rural District Council Meeting and only three members voted in favour of members' expenses being paid.

Damage and loss estimated at about £800 was caused by a serious fire in February at the bakery of the Bridgwater Co-operative Society at Edward Street. The firemen were hampered in their work when the floor of the store above collapsed and a large quantity of flour fell down.

In June a fire occurred at the chair manufacturing premises of Kraft Productions, Ltd., and damage estimated at between £4,000 and £5,000 was caused. Nearly one hundred workmen were temporarily unemployed.

On the night of Saturday, 24 August, Bridgwater had its first visit from Nazi bombers. Firemen fighting a blaze at a brick and tile works were machine-gunned and several people were killed by direct hits on a row of houses.

The Bridgwater Police Force was amalgamated with the Somerset County Constabulary on 1 October. The force comprised Chief Constable, Inspector, four Sergeants, and 14 Constables.

Much attention was given to matters arising out of war-time conditions. The 'Grow more Food' and 'Dig for Victory' campaigns were given greater prominence.

Large numbers of children and adults were evacuated under the Government's scheme and were billeted in the town and district.

The presence of large numbers of troops in the town caused the Council to provide entertainment for them. A Committee was formed and organised concerts in the Town Hall; many local entertainers willingly came forward to take part in the programmes. The concerts were well patronised and greatly appreciated by the soldiers, and the Hall was crowded on every occasion. The old *Palace* theatre was also utilised as a social centre for the troops.

The Mayor was Mr Robert Ashton.

1941 'Brighter Bridgwater' was the slogan which resulted after the appearance of floral baskets on the Cornhill Dome.

War-time tasks worthily achieved dominated the life of Bridgwater during the year. The year began with a big National Savings drive. 'War Weapons Week' followed and later there was a 'Warship Week'.

The Mayor was Mr Robert Ashton.

1942 Damage caused by a fire at the premises of Whitby, Light & Lane in George Street, was estimated at over £1,000.

The population of the town was 17,586.

'Digging for Victory' and 'Saving for Victory' were the two duties of greatest importance and were the mainsprings of endeavour in the town and district.

Early in the year a 'British Restaurant' was opened in St John's Hall, Monmouth Street, and was well patronised by both workers and other townspeople. The excellent meals and service were greatly appreciated.

The Mayor was Mr Robert Ashton.

1943 Abnormally low unemployment figures were presented at Bridgwater in March. They were: Bridgewater, 11 people out of work; Highbridge, nine; and Street, four.

The Glass Cone was demolished in 1943.

Several thousand pounds' worth of damage was caused by fire at the Monmouth Street butchery and grocery shops of the Co-operative Society.

The Mayor was Mr Harold Scholfield.

1944 The town and district contributed to the National Savings movement and during the 'Salute the Soldier' week the target of £350,000 was easily beaten and a grand total of £404,767 was reached.

Bridgwater was visited by a thunderstorm of unusual severity on Whit Tuesday. It was described as the longest and most severe in living memory, and considerable damage was caused to crops in the rural area.

A large contingent of American forces was billeted in the town and district—jeeps becoming an everyday sight. The town extended warm hospitality to its overseas visitors which was amply appreciated by the American soldiers.

The Mayor was Mr Robert Chamberlain.

1945 At the General Election held in June, the result was as follows:

Mr Vernon Bartlett (Independent)	17,937
Major Gerald Wills (Conservative)	15,625
Mr N. Corkhill (Labour)	5,613

(Independent majority, 2,312)

One of the oldest inns in Bridgwater, the *Three Crowns* in St Mary Street, was damaged by fire. Prompt action by the Fire Brigade saved the building from serious harm.

A plaque was erected in Westminster Abbey in memory of Admiral Robert Blake. Among those present at the dedication ceremony were the Mayor, Lieut-Col. R. Chamberlain, the Vicar of Bridgwater, Preb. E. H. Hughes-Davies, and the M.P. for Bridgwater, Mr Vernon Bartlett.

The most memorable day of the whole year was Tuesday, 8 May, when Mr Winston Churchill announced to the nation that hostilities in Europe were at an end. The news, though not unexpected, let loose a flood of rejoicing, and there were jubilant scenes on the Cornhill and in other parts of the town.

The Mayor was Mr Robert Chamberlain.

1946 The Arts Centre in Castle Street, the first of its kind in Britain, was opened by the Arts Council of Great Britain. Its purpose was to bring together all those who had a lively interest in music, drama and painting. It is a delightful early Georgian house and the interior decoration is simple, modern and effective. The hall and rooms are let for a variety of purposes.

Bridgwater Guy Fawkes Carnival was revived on Thursday, 7 November, after a lapse of seven years, and brought with it some of its pre-war glory. What was believed to be a record number of people witnessed the procession and squibbing display.

In August fires of a serious nature occurred at two factories in the town. Damage estimated at over £1,000 was caused at Messrs H. F. Tottle's works at Bristol Road. Employees of Crypton Equipment successfully tackled an outbreak at their factory and by their efforts prevented the fire from assuming large proportions, and saved it spreading to the adjoining premises of Berry & Co., wholesale grocers.

In June work commenced on C. & J. Clark's factory, when a grandson of Field-Marshal Smuts cut the first turf on the site.

In June an outstanding event was the celebration of St John's Church centenary. A copper beech tree was planted by the Bishop of Bath and Wells, Dr H. W. Bradbeer, to mark the occasion.

The Mayor was Mr Robert Chamberlain.

1947 On 27 January the new factory of C. & J. Clark, Ltd., boot and shoe manufacturers, was opened.

At the end of January the town had one of the heaviest snowfalls for many years, in the middle of one of the longest winters of the century. February was a very cold month, and the Docks were frozen over and vessels were unable to enter or leave for some days. Tons of snow was cleared from the streets and in country districts many homes were cut off by deep drifts.

In May crops were severely damaged by a severe thunderstorm which was stated to be one of the worst in living memory.

In June a unique honour was the announcement that Father F. J. Grimshaw, whose parents lived in Cranleigh Gardens, was to be the new Roman Catholic Bishop of Plymouth.

A big fire occurred in August when the Great Western Railway sheets department in Colley Lane was swept by flames that could be seen 10 miles away.

In October the new factory of Plaster Products (Greenhithe), Ltd., was opened at Dunball by the Minister of Works, the Right Hon C. W. Key, M.P.

It was made known during the month of December that Halesleigh Tower, a large residence off Wembdon Road had been sold to a local firm who had turned it into an inn.

The Mayor was Mr Robert Washer.

1948 In May a new factory, Messrs Crypton Equipment, Ltd., was opened in the presence of a representative gathering of industrialists.

A very severe thunderstorm broke out in the early hours of the last day in July. The thunderclaps, resembling heavy gunfire, kept people awake throughout most of the night. Cattle were killed by lightning.

The Mayor was Mr Robert Washer.

1949 In February Mr Sidney G. Jarman, author of *Jarman's History of Bridgwater* died at his home, 7 Haytor Road, Wrexham, North Wales. He was in his 93rd year. News of his death was received with much regret by his friends in Bridgwater, particularly by members of the Loyal Halswell Lodge (No. 3975) Independent Order of Oddfellows, of which he was the oldest member, having joined the Order 66 years before. Mr Jarman, who was a journalist, left Bridgwater many years before to make his home in Wrexham, where he had the honour of being mayor on two occasions, and from where he received the Freedom of the Borough.

In June, owing to the drought, the water shortage in Bridgwater became very serious, and an order was enforced prohibiting the use of water for gardening purposes, or for car- and footpath-washing.

A big fire occurred at the Church Street premises of C. J. Harris (Bridgwater), Ltd., manufacturers of animal feeding stuffs.

In October a disastrous fire, causing thousands of pounds worth of damage broke out at the Devonshire Street Factory of Kingsley Art Furniture, Ltd., owned by Alderman Edward Wills.

A house in Castle Street was acquired as the new headquarters of the local branch of the British Legion. Mr Vernon Bartlett, M.P., emphasised the need for the British Legion at the annual county conference.

'Any Questions', the popular West Country radio programme was broadcast from King Street Methodist Hall.

The Mayor was Mr Robert Washer.

1950 The main hall of the Town Hall was completely modernised when a new floor was constructed, together with a new stage with modern lighting arrangements. The proscenium was specially commissioned to suit the new scheme and the whole hall was redecorated in bright colours.

At the General Election held on 23 February the result was as follows:

Major Gerald Wills (Conservative)	21,732
Mr Norman Carr (Labour)	16,053
Mr Stephen King-Hall (Independent)	6,708

(Conservative majority, 5,679)

Jarman's candle factory in Clare Street closed down. This was an old family business started by Charles Jarman in 1870. He married a niece of William Bowering who owned the property and at his death in 1877 she inherited it.

The Mayor was Mr Edward Wills.

1951 A disastrous fire occurred at Messrs Waddon's Rope Walk which led to its closure and the subsequent disposal of the site to the Bridgwater Corporation.

The population of Bridgwater was 22,221.

At the General Election held on 25 October the result was as follows:

Mr Gerald Wills (Conservative)	25,365
Mr Norman Carr (Labour)	19,656

(Conservative majority, 5,709)

The Mayor was Mr Edward Wills.

1952 By the Bridgwater (Extension) Order, 1952, the Borough of Bridgwater was extended to include parts of the Parish of Bridgwater Without, Durleigh, and North Petherton.

On a wintry night at the end of January the last passenger train left Bridgwater for Edington on the old Somerset and Dorset railway line from Bridgwater North Station, after which the station was closed.

In February the Mayor, Councillor P. Wills, was presented with Bridgwater's new coat-of-arms, recently granted to the Borough by the College of Heralds. The Deputy Mayor, Councillor Edward Wills, who launched the fund for the coat-of-arms in 1951 said the cost had been met by the loyal citizens of the town.

In March a big fire occurred at the Puriton Ordnance factory. The police canteen was almost entirely destroyed. The glow in the sky could be seen for miles around.

1953 The Church of the Good Shepherd, Greenfield, Hamp Street, was dedicated by the Bishop of Bath and Wells.

In June the buildings and streets were gaily decorated in honour of the memorable occasion of the coronation of Her Majesty Queen Elizabeth II. A loyal message to Her Majesty was sent by the Mayor, Mr G. N. Hayball, on behalf of the people of the town. Bridgwater responded well to the call to attend a united service at St Mary's Church on the Sunday preceding the coronation in which all denominations and practically every organisation in the Borough participated. The Church was filled to overflowing and prayers were offered for the Queen that she may be sustained and fortified throughout her life for the high task to which she had been called. In all main streets and side roads, from public buildings and shops hung flags, pennants and bunting in a blaze of colour in honour of the young Queen. The ancient town and surrounding villages thus celebrated the occasion in loyal fashion.

Alderman Walter Deacon, an ex-mayor, was presented with the Freedom of the Borough on 5 November.

The Mayor was Mr George N. Hayball.

1954 The Right Rev Joseph Grimshaw, Roman Catholic Bishop of Plymouth, and native of Bridgwater, was appointed the new Archbishop of Birmingham.

In October while Bridgwater firemen were ensuring the safety of the premises of Kraft Productions, Ltd., following a fire, an outbreak of a more serious nature was discovered at another industrial establishment, the joinery works of Messrs H. F. Tottle & Sons, Ltd., less than a mile away.

The Mayor was Mr A. B. John.

1955 At the General Election held on 26 May the result was as follows:

Mr Gerald Wills (Conservative)	24,887
Mr Sumner (Labour)	17,170

(Conservative majority, 7,717)

The Bridgwater Mercury celebrated its centenary with the issue of 21 June. During this 100 years Bridgwater had become much less reliant on shipping and agriculture, and was much more heavily industralised.

The Mayor was Mr Raymond Biddiscombe.

1956 The population of Bridgwater was 23,700.

Heavy damage was caused in a fire which almost destroyed the premises of Lane & Co. (Stationers), in George Street.

A serious outbreak of fire occurred at Malvern Cottage, Taunton Road, the home of Mr and Mrs Frank Mawdsley; they escaped by climbing down a drainpipe in their night attire.

The Mayor was Mr Norman R. Gray.

1957 In January a fire occurred at the furniture factory of Squibbs Ltd., in Mount Street. Two assembly shops, covering about 2,000 square feet were gutted. Prompt work by the Bridgwater Fire Brigade prevented the fire from spreading to the rest of the factory buildings. It was during the lunch hour that the outbreak was discovered. Damage was estimated at several thousand pounds.

In August a disastrous fire occurred at Bowering's cattle food mill at Moat Lane. People left their houses to watch one of the most spectacular fires in the town for a long time. Damage estimated at thousands of pounds was caused by the flames which were seen for miles around the town.

A start had been made on the world's largest atomic power station at Hinkley Point, and the magnificent approach road was completed in a remarkably short space of time.

The Mayor was Mr William Oscar Coate.

1958 The last service took place at Holy Trinity Church, Taunton Road, prior to its demolition.

On 29 March the new relief road and bridge, known as 'Broadway' and 'Blake Bridge' were opened by the Mayor of Bridgwater. The new road is 530 yards long and has an overall width of 74ft. There are two 20ft. carriageways with a 4ft. central strip and footpaths on either side of 15ft. The bridge, which is constructed of reinforced concrete, is 160ft. long, with a centre span of 70ft. and two side spans of 45ft. Hundreds of people attended the ceremony, including some who had seen the Town Bridge opened 75 years before. The ceremony was preceded by a civic luncheon at the Town Hall.

The General Post Office was transferred to the Corn Exchange on the Cornhill.

Heavy damage was caused when fire gutted Messrs Biddick's furniture workshop in Clare Street. Flames rose to 40ft. and adjoining houses were evacuated, but local fire brigades averted a major disaster.

July saw the opening of Ivy House, Friarn Street, a home for elderly people. The ceremony was performed by the Deputy-Mayor, Alderman W. O. Coate, who had been actively associated with the project and whose broadcast appeal for funds had resulted in the subscription of substantial sums.

Alderman E. J. Davies, believed to be the Borough's youngest Mayor, was installed this year.

1959 At the General Election on 8 October, the result was as follows:

Mr Gerald Wills (Conservative)	23,002
Mr J. Finnigan (Labour)	14,706
Mr P. J. Watkins (Liberal)	7,893

(Conservative majority, 8,296)

Preb. E. H. Hughes-Davis, Vicar of Bridgwater, was presented with the Freedom of the Borough on his retirement.

The water shortage was so acute at one time during the summer that it was feared that rationing by the use of standpipes in the streets might have to be introduced.

The provision of a new civic centre was stressed as an urgent necessity at a meeting of the Town Council. It was estimated that the building would cost £250,000, though further plans were never developed.

The first woman to hold the office of Mayor, Alderman Mrs A. B. Potterton, was elected.

1960 A big fire causing estimated damage of £20,000 occurred at the brick and tile factory of John Board & Co. (Bridgwater), Ltd.

This year was probably the wettest of the century, and thousands of acres of land in the town and district were waterlogged.

A stage in the development of Bridgwater's trading estate at Colley Lane was the opening of the new factory of Wills Pressure Filled Joint Ring, Ltd., at a cost of nearly £20,000.

Work began on a new Church at Greenfield, with a seating capacity of 300, designed to replace Holy Trinity Church.

The opening ceremony of the New Broadway Lido, the town's long-awaited new swimming baths, was performed by the Mayor, Alderman Mrs A. B. Potterton.

A major road improvement, the extension of the dual carriageway of the internal relief road, at a cost of £50,000, took place in Monmouth Street.

Messrs Wellworthy, Ltd., purchased the factory at Colley Lane formerly occupied by Wilmot Breeden, Ltd.

The Mayor was Mr J. G. Headford (who died in office) followed by Mrs A. B. Potterton.

1961 Many new streets were built in the town and it is of interest to recall the origin of the names of some of the present streets. Penel Orlieu is an unusual name. It recalls two streets: Penel, well-known in medieval times; and Orlieu, from a family of the name of Orloue. Castle Street was once known as Chandos Street; and the present Chandos Street was Little Chandos Street, both named from the family of the Duke of Buckingham, who built them in the 18th century. Castle Bailey refers to the courtyard of the medieval Castle. Friarn Street derives its name from the Franciscan Friary, founded in the 13th century. Horse Pond, off Friarn Street, was used for centuries for watering horses in Durleigh Brook; Moat Lane took its name from the town moat where it ran from the West Gate to Durleigh Brook, but Moat Lane has now been buried under Broadway.

In October the water shortage was making news; the position was serious and the supply was cut off from 10.30 p.m. to 6 a.m. On 7 November a report stated 'The level at Durleigh Reservoir is now only four inches higher than at the height of the drought in 1959'.

On 21 November the water shortage worsened and water was cut off from 9 p.m. to 6.30 a.m.

Workmen in the *Rose and Crown* inn uncovered a large open hearth fireplace with massive oak beams. The bar now occupies the site of the hearth beneath a huge black beam. Alongside the fireplace was a traditional bread oven, moulded chiefly from clay set on a stone shelf. This has been preserved alongside the bar.

The building which stood here in 1300 is known to have been the house of a merchant, but the oven is not as old as that.

The new Church of Holy Trinity at Greenfield was consecrated by the Lord Bishop of Bath and Wells, the Right Rev Dr E. B. Henderson.

Bridgwater's 2,000th post-war council house was officially opened by the Minister of Housing and Local Government, Sir Keith Joseph, Bart., M.P.

In July there was a visit to the town by H.R.H. Princess Alexandra. Thousands of people came to the town to catch a glimpse of her.

The population of Bridgwater was 26,300.

The Mayor was Mr A. D. Frost.

1962 The Minister of Health's decision to close the local hospital brought a storm of protest. The Minister stated that the hospital was to become a unit for the treatment of the aged and chronically sick, after the building of a new hospital at Taunton in 1975.

Bridgwater was by 1962 one of the largest towns in the south-west of England.

A big fire occurred in February at Mount Radford, Wembdon, a large mansion. More than half the house was destroyed, making five families temporarily homeless. The blaze could be seen for many miles.

The Hawkridge Reservoir at Spaxton was opened by Sir George McNaughton, President of the Institute of Civil Engineers. The reservoir cost £600,000.

In July the new Sydenham County Secondary School was officially opened. The school which includes playing fields and a caretaker's house, cost £187,000, and is one of the best equipped in the country.

The Mayor was Mr C. W. Milne.

1963 'The Town Council have made Bridgwater the laughing stock of the country' was what the Rev E. A. E. Gill said when criticising their refusal to permit the Boy Scouts' flag to fly over the Cornhill Buildings on the occasion of the Somerset County Jamboree, at Stockland, at Whitsuntide. His statement made front-page news in *The Bridgwater Mercury,* and was splashed in the national press, and was broadcast in radio bulletins.

In March, news of a takeover bid by Banbury Buildings, Ltd., for Coate's Fencing, Ltd., was announced.

A new school, the St Joseph's Roman Catholic Primary School, situated between Quantock Road and Park Road was built, costing over £50,000. It was officially opened in May 1964 by the Bishop of Clifton, the Right Rev Joseph Rudderham.

The winter of 1963 was one of the coldest and most severe for almost 80 years. There were phenomenally heavy falls of snow, sub-zero temperatures, and hard frosts. Many villages were cut off, hundreds of people were snowbound, bus and rail services were disrupted, and thousands of water pipes froze.

June saw the opening of a new bank, Martin's Bank, in the High Street.

In April a £27,000 factory, which Bridgwater Town Council had built for Herb-Royal, Ltd., on the Colley Lane Estate, was officially opened by the Mayor, Alderman G. C. Harris.

The Borough's new Red Cross Centre, at the junction of Broadway and Taunton Road, was officially opened.

A fire occured in the spraying department of the furniture factory of R. Slocombe & Sons, Ltd., in Monmouth Street. It caused damage estimated at several thousand pounds.

The new Post Office supplies department in Bristol Road was opened. It cost £200,000, and was built in 10 months.

1964 Bridgwater's new Fire Station was opened in November by the Somerset County Council Chairman, Lieut.-Col. G. C. G. Grey. It cost £64,780.

At the General Election held on 15 October, the result was as follows:

Sir Gerald Wills (Conservative)	20,822
Mr P. Hart (Labour)	14,645
Mr P. Watkins (Liberal)	9,009
Mr M. Hart (Independent)	2,038

(Conservative majority, 6,177)

Traffic wardens made their appearance in Bridgwater streets for the first time.

A spectacular fire occurred at G. Randle & Sons, timber merchants, at the Docks, which caused thousands of pounds' worth of damage. Hundreds of people flocked to the Docks to watch it, and it could be seen for miles.

The Northgate Brewery of Messrs Starkey, Knight and Ford, Ltd., ceased to brew locally and was closed down. The Company had about 450 public houses in Somerset and Devon, with breweries at Bridgwater and Tiverton, but it is now part of the Whitbread organisation. The end of the Northgate Brewery was a matter of regret for many townspeople.

The dual carriageway extension of Broadway which links Taunton Road with Penel Orlieu was opened in February.

In April a new Community Centre was opened at Sydenham at a cost of £13,000.

In May Alderman Mrs Beatrice Davis was installed as the second woman Mayoress in the town's municipal history.

1965 In March there was a big fire at the Huntworth Gate Garage, damage amounting to thousands of pounds.

Mr Arthur Wevell, formerly Headmaster of Westover Boys' School, was made a Freeman of the Borough. He was the fifth person to be so honoured.

A £400,000 takeover of the Quantock Preserving Company's premises at Wembdon Road was made by James Robertson, Ltd., the country's biggest jam and marmalade manufacturers, in May.

Damage totalling several thousands of pounds was caused by a Sunday morning fire in August at Swayne's shoe-repairing factory in Eastover.

The appeal in October by the Rector of Spaxton and Charlynch, the Rev Geoffrey Watkins Grubb, against his deprivation of a living was dismissed by the Church Court. A notice was pinned on the Cathedral door at Wells by the Bishop declaring the joint parishes vacant.

The largest public meeting anyone at Wembdon could remember took place in February in the Church Room, at which a unanimous resolution opposing 'by every possible means' the incorporation of Wembdon as part of the Borough of Bridgwater, was passed.

Bridgwater's first 'skyscraper' block of flats in West Street was officially opened by the Mayor, Alderman Mrs B. M. Davis.

The Arts Centre in Castle Street was purchased in June by the Bridgwater Corporation and is now let to the Bridgwater and District Arts Guild.

1966 At the General Election held on 31 March the result was as follows:

Sir Gerald Wills (Conservative)	20,850
Mr Richard Mayer (Labour)	17,864
Mr Philip Watkins (Liberal)	8,205

(Conservative majority, 2,986)

The Hinkley Point Nuclear Power Station was officially opened by the Minister of Power, Mr Richard Marsh, M.P. A lavish reception was laid on for 500 guests.

One of the heaviest April snowfalls in living memory gave the area a Christmas-card appearance in Easter week. It lay to a depth of 4ins. in Bridgwater, and 6ins. in some of the surrounding villages.

Bridgwater's new Police headquarters, erected at a cost of £117,000, was officially opened by the Lord Lieutenant of Somerset, Lord Hylton, in May.

Bridgwater was hit by the worst thunderstorm in memory. Every available pump was called in to deal with the flooding. One and a half inches of rain fell in 40 minutes and almost every road in the town was flooded.

In October the new £55,000 Westfield Congregational Church (now United Reformed) was opened.

A freak whirlwind suddenly tore across the south of the town on 1 December. It left an extensive trail of damage to homes and public buildings including the Fire Station, the Gas Works and 30 council houses. Amazingly, no serious injuries were reported.

The new Chilton Trinity School, which stands on the outskirts of the town in Chilton Street, was opened.

The Mayor was Mr E. J. Davies.

1967 'Overspill' was the headline at the beginning of the year when the Town Clerk, Mr John Turner, presented a report to the Borough Council and warned that any newcomers to Bridgwater would have to be made welcome.

The Town Council decided not to buy Bridgwater's 100-year-old Docks when they heard that they would be letting themselves in for a deficit of £7,000 a year.

The town's new Bus Station was opened in East Quay on the site of old properties that were demolished several years ago. It was described as one of the best of its kind in the country.

Work started on the second nuclear power station at Hinkley Point at an estimated cost of £94 million.

In October the Mayor, Mr Louis Steer, one of the Borough's most popular chief citizens, died.

The Carnival in November provided a most magnificent display and the procession was seen by thousands.

At the end of the year heavy snow and icy roads caused considerable traffic chaos, but in the town the snow was quickly cleared to keep traffic moving.

The Registrar General's estimated population of the Borough was 26,580.

The Mayor was Mr Louis Steer (who died in office), followed by Mr G. C. Harris.

95. The river with sailing vessels approaching the town with the spire of St. Mary's church in the distance. One of the sketches made by John Chubb in 1790.

96. The old Stone Bridge over the River Parrett, a sketch by John Chubb, *c.*1790.

97. The Cornhill and St Mary's church steeple, one of John Chubb's sketches, showing old shops and houses long since demolished.

98. The old High Cross on the Cornhill, sketched by John Chubb. The cross was erected in the 14th century, and used as a Market for the sale of many articles, including fish, butter, cheese and vegetables. It was the centre where the whole town gathered to buy and sell, to gossip and to hear the news; during election times and in public rejoicing. In 1685 the ill-fated Duke of Monmouth was proclaimed King before it. It bore the motto 'Mind your own business'. The Cross was pulled down after the erection of the first Market Hall under the Act of 1779 but the date of its demolition was not recorded.

9. (*top*) The ruins of Bridgwater 'astle from a sketch made by John :hubb, *c.*1800. It was built between ıe years 1200 and 1210 by Lord 'illiam Brewer. It has long since een destroyed with the exception f the water-gate at the West Quay. he walls were said to be 15 ft. in ıickness and over 20 ft. high.

00. (*centre*) A sketch by John hubb showing what was left of ıe 'Island', a row of houses in the ıiddle of the High Street. Their emolition was completed in 1856 nd it was thought that this would e a great improvement to the eighbourhood as the High Street 'ould then be as wide a street as ad any town in the west of ngland. The row of narrow houses egan originally at the Cornhill and ın as far as the Mansion House.

01. (*bottom*) The old North Gate, ;etched by John Chubb. The North ate stood at the end of a rough .ne which later was to become ngel Crescent. The arch became angerous and the whole thing was ılled down in 1798.

The BRITANNIA.

Launched at the Port of Bridgwater, on Saturday, September **24. 1831.**

RULE BRITANNIA.

When Britain first, at Heaven's command,
Arose from out the azure Main,
This was the Charter of the Land,
And Guardian Angels sung this strain,

Rule Britannia! Britannia Rule the Waves!
Britons never will be Slaves.

The Nations not so blest as thee,
Must, in their turn, to Tyrants fall;
Whilst thou shalt flourish, great and free,
The dread and glory of them all.

Rule Britannia. &c.

Still more Majestic thou shalt rise,
More dreadful from each foreign stroke;
As the loud blast, that rends the skies,
Serves but to root thy Native *Oak.*

Rule Britannia, &c.

Thee, haughty Tyrants ne'er shall tame,
All their attempts to bind thee down;
Will but arouze thy gen'rous flame,
And work their woe, and thy renown.

Rule Britannia, &c.

To thee belongs the rural reign;
Thy Cities shall with Commerce shine;
All thine shall be the subject Main,
And ev'ry shore it circles, thine.

Rule Britannia, &c.

The Muses, still with Freedom found,
Shall to thy happy coast repair;
Blest Isle! with matchless beauty crown'd,
And manly hearts to guard the Fair.

Rule Britannia! Britannia Rule the Waves!
Britons never will be Slaves.

102. (*left*) The ship *Britannia* which was built and launched at the Port of Bridgwater in September 1831.

103. (*below*) The south side of High Street in 1865. The *White Lion Inn* with the horse-drawn waggon with large barrels probably containing cider brought into the town by a local farmer. Very little traffic about; note the lady in the crinoline dress and the lads with long trousers and peaked caps.

St. Mary Street about 1864.

104. (*above*) Old houses and shops, for-
nerly 'The Shambles' on the north side
of the High Street. The building line was
never advanced when the western part of
'the island' had finally gone, unlike the
louses on the right which had all been
ebuilt and advanced by several feet. The
vide pavement still shows what the true
width of the High Street should have
been.

105. (*right*) St Mary Street looking
towards St Mary's church in 1865. The
black-faced clock on the tower of the
church which was removed in 1867 and
replaced by a new clock can be seen. A
quiet and peaceful street compared with
the busy thoroughfare today. Note the
three-wheeled child's go-cart as they were
then called, and the lady with the crinoline. Most of the lads wore peaked caps
and long trousers.

106. The Old Town Bridge from Salmon Parade, formerly called Salmon Lane, in 1865.

107. The Dome and Market House buildings in 1865. The railings in front of the building were eventually removed on 20 September 1895.

8. St Mary's church from the Cornhill in 1865.

109. A picture of the Old Vestry of St Mary's church with its conical roof, in 1865. In 1902 the present Vestry was built, replacing this old one which was much too small and in a bad state of repair.

110. The river at Crowpill in 1865 on a wintry day with snow lying about. The *Hope and Anchor Inn*, now closed, is on the left. A large brick kiln, now demolished, is in the distance. The large chestnut trees from Crowpill House (also now demolished) overhang the west bank of the river. A crane on the west bank has now been removed.

111. A view of the east side of King Square in 1865. The balconies on the first floor have been removed. Some boys standing on the corner are dressed in long trousers and peaked caps. The rough stony road would be dusty in the summer and muddy in winter.

112. The old *Rose and Crown Inn* at the corner of St Mary Street and Friarn Street in 1865.

113. Houses in Castle Street in 1865. The road was of cobble-stones with guttering through the centre. In 1723 a local builder, Benjamin Holloway, who was employed by the Duke of Chandos, began to build these houses. Holloway also built houses in Chandos Street. Castle Street was originally called Chandos Street and Chandos Street was called Little Chandos Street.

114. The beautiful residence, 'The Lions', at West Quay, in 1865. It was then the residence of Mr William Browne who was Mayor of the town in 1854. Later it was the home of Mr W. T. Holland who was Mayorin 1879 and 1880, and after that Mr Foley of the Somerset Trading Company lived there. The house was built by Benjamin Holloway in about 1730.

115. Penel Orlieu House (No. 1 York Buildings) at the back of the *Royal Clarence Hotel* in 1865, when it was a private house. Renamed 'The Mart' it has been much altered and now contains offices. However, the facade is still recognisable, but the garden is a private car park.

116. 'The Willows', Taunton Road, in 1865. This fine old residence at the bottom of Ashleigh Avenue is still standing. There have been quite a number of different occupiers over the years and it still retains its dignified appearance, but it has been divided into two houses.

117. Crowpill House, West Quay, in 1865, now demolished. A fine old residence which was at one time occupied by Mr Sully of the firm of Shippers and Coal Factors.

18. Brent Lodge, Taunton Road in 1865, now the site of a petrol filling station, Nos. 9-11 aunton Road, at the junction of Broadway and Taunton Road, close to the traffic lights.

119. Westfield House, West Street, in 1865. It was demolished in 1966 and the new Westfield United Reformed church built on the site. It was the residence of the late Mr F. H. Allen who was Mayor of the town in 1922.

120. Penel Orlieu in 1865 with the *Mason's Arms Inn* on the right and the *Three Tuns Inn* in the centre, before the Cattle Market was built and opened in 1877. It is now the site of the Classic Theatre.

121. Dampiet Street at the junction of Blake Street and George Street looking towards St Mary Street in 1865. A large chestnut tree overhangs the footpath from Dampiet House on the right. The Unitarian Chapel is on the left.

122. Taunton Road looking towards the town in 1865. The large house on the left was the residence of the late Mr Symons, a brick and tile manufacturer.

123. The north side of King Square in 1865. There were then large gates at the exit into Northgate which were closed at times.

124. (*left*) St Mary's church in 1867 showing the Old Vestry which was replaced by the present Vestry in 1902. In 1902 the two oak screens in the church (one on the west side of the organ and the other forming the entrance to the Memorial chapel) were fixed. Electric light was also installed in this year.

125. (*below*) A view of the River Parrett at Saltlands with St John's church in the distance and a long length of landing berths. This view was taken in the winter of 1870 with ice and snow in the river and on the banks. Practically all trace of the wooden staging has now been removed.

126. The Cattle Market and part of Penel Orlieu soon after its opening in 1875. It is now the site of the Classic Cinema and car park. The town was a busy market centre for the surrounding agricultural district. Large weekly markets of cattle, pigs and horses were held.

27. Members of the Bridgwater Cycling Club outside the *Bristol Arms Hotel* in 1881. One of he most popular events was the Cycling Club's annual athletic sports which took place during the nonth of August. The sports were held in a field not far from the *Malt Shovel Hotel.* Interest was ot confined to Bridgwater and competitors came from as far away as Guernsey, Southampton, oventry, Cardiff and Bournemouth. The programme began at 1.30 p.m. and ran on late into the vening.

128. A view of Bridgwater Hospital in 1883 when there was an exceptionally high tide, flooding the West and East Quays, Binford Place, Salmon Parade and Eastover. Water can be seen at the entrance to the Hospital. In 1883 a flood bank known as Baltmoor Wall in the Athelney district broke in three places and caused flooding up to a depth of eight feet. The railway between Bridgwater and Durston was flooded causing great inconvenience. The loss to farmers and others was very considerable.

129. Decorations at the junction of the Bristol and Bath roads on the occasion of the Bath and West of England Agricultural Show in 1883.

130. The Union Workhouse, Northgate, in 1890. The neat, white stone building, now demolished, was erected in 1837 at a cost of £9,000 and could accommodate 388 people. At the back there was a hospital now known as Blake Hospital. The Union then consisted of 40 parishes and the Guardians met every Wednesday in the Boardroom. The site of this entrance building is now occupied by the Enterprise Centre for the Handicapped.

131. The south side of Eastover in 1890.

132. A photograph taken in 1897 of the great Glass Cone built *c.*1720 for the Duke of Chandos. No glass was made there after 1729 but it was converted into a kiln to fire coarse pots and (in the 20th century) tiles. It was a most inefficient kiln and was demolished in 1943. The base, with walls standing several feet high, is to be preserved as a fragment of industrial archaeology.

133. A view of the Canal and Docks in 1898. The British Oil & Cake Mills are on the left and a large kiln is on the right. On the night of 26 February 1893 a great fire occurred at the Oil & Cake Mills and damage ran into tens of thousands of pounds. It was Bridgwater's most spectacular fire but miraculously no-one was injured.

134. The River Parrett from West Quay in 1898. Fishing boats are on the bank; a vessel is in the dry dock of Carver & Sons; and ships are moored at each side of the river up to the Town Bridge.

135. A horse brake outing, probably to Holford and Kilve or Burnham-on-Sea, from the *Punch Bowl Inn*, West Quay, in about 1902. These outings were then very popular and most enjoyable with mountains of food and mugs of foaming English ale. The homeward journey was the best part of the day.

136. The Town Bridge and Fore Street in 1902 with horse-drawn traffic and cyclists. Nelson's Ltd., butchers, had premises at the corner of Fore Street and Binford Place. The population of Bridgwater was about 15,000, and as can be seen from the picture, it was a thriving town, full of enterprise and energy. The trade of the port was brisk and local industries, particularly the brick and tile trade were in full swing and the local tradesmen had not much reason to complain of dullness of trade.

137. High Street in 1905 with the cab stand in the middle of the street. The *Royal Clarence Hotel* and Taylor's Restaurant are on the right.

More Pictures of Old Bridgwater

138. (*above*) Alexandra Place, Now Alexandra Road, in 1865, with a view of the first four or five houses to be built. On the left is the wall of the original *Malt Shovel Inn* which was demolished in 1904, and beyond that the entrance to Victoria Road. Note the rough state of the road, typically dusty and stony in summer and dirty and muddy in winter; tar macadam had not been invented. The rest of the houses in Alexandra Road were built soon after 1865.

139. (*right*) A picture of Hamp House, in 1865, known locally as 'Paul Reed's' because Mr Paul Reed, a well-known local solicitor lived there at one time. It is a beautiful residence which looks to date from the Georgian period, with large grounds and many trees.

140. Shop premises at the corner of West Street and North Street in 1902, known as Gardener's Dining Rooms, decorated for the occasion of the Coronation of King Edward VII. Hot dinners were 6d. and 8d; plain teas were 6d; a cup of tea, coffee or cocoa cost 1d. 'Fry's Chocolate' notices were much in evidence in the windows. At one time this part of the town was known as 'West Bow'. This old property has been demolished. The site, together with that of the adjoining houses is now taken by 'West Bow House', a large block of old people's flats.

141. Postmen outside the Post Office in the High Street in 1904. In 1848 the Post Office was in St Mary Street and was managed by Alfred Saunders. Letters were delivered in the town daily at 7 a.m., 10 a.m. and 5.20 p.m. Letters could be posted until 10 p.m. for delivery to London the next morning and postage cost 1d. Later the Post Office was moved to East Quay, then to the High Street and thence to the Cornhill.

142. The original *West India House Inn*, Durleigh Road, in 1865. The proprietress and her children are sitting outside the old thatched building. In those days there were large numbers of beer and cider houses and it is presumed that the proprietor went out to work in addition to keeping a licensed house. In some cases they made their own beer and cider. Of course, there were then very few houses in Durleigh, it was mostly farms and farm cottages.

143. Decorations in St Mary Street on the occasion of the visit of the Bath and West of England Agricultural Show to the town in 1883. Nearly every street was decorated in a similar manner and a large amount of enterprise and enthusiasm was displayed by the townspeople throughout a week in May. The attendance of visitors at the show far exceeded expectations. On the right is Poole's Provision Warehouse, cheese factor and manufacturer of the celebrated Bridgwater sausages.

144. Decorations on the Cornhill for the occasion of the Coronation of King Edward VII in 1902. The celebrations in August were very elaborate and highly successful. The main features were a wholesale distribution of half-crown tickets among the aged poor and specially-struck medals to all school children in the town. The Cornhill was lavishly beflagged and artistically decorated, as were the main thoroughfares. There was a procession and fete with several bands in attendance. It was a big meeting during which loyal greetings were sent from the townspeople of Bridgwater to His Majesty.

145. A steamer called the *Premier* in the Docks in 1902. Although when this picture was taken, shipping was in decline, still quite a large number of ships made use of the Docks. This Dock was opened on 25 March 1841 and a public holiday was declared to celebrate the occasion.

146. The launching of a lifeboat which may have been for Burnham on the East Quay in 1890. The occasion was celebrated by a large number of spectators from both sides of the river. The lifeboat is actually just about to drop into the water. There are some people in the lifeboat and some small boats on the river watching the proceedings in case of a mishap. Presumably the lifeboat was built at Carver's shipyard at the East Quay and is being launched just near Messrs Bradford's premises.

147. A view of North Street looking towards the *Malt Shovel Inn* in 1904, when it was rebuilt. On the left were Acland's shops, Stationers, Printers, Newsagents and Tobacconists. On the right were shops and Miss Everdale's School for girls, now the site of Messrs A. & S. White, service station and car showrooms. There was practically no traffic about. The picture was obviously taken on a bright sunny day as the sun blinds were out over the shop fronts.

148. The east side of King Square in 1865. All the houses in King Square were then, as now, occupied by local business or professional gentlemen. The corner building on the left was Miss Johnson's School for boys and girls, now occupied by the Ministry of Labour. The gardens were surrounded by railings with entrance gates, and the square was a pleasant and restful spot in the centre of the town. The pupils of the school took their exercise in the gardens. Most of the houses had cellars, balconies and shutters on the windows.

149. The River Parrett frozen over during the hard winter of 1895. It was an exceptionally hard winter and during the cold spell of February bonfires were lit on the frozen river, people fried pancakes and had tea parties on the frozen river at Moorland and Somerset Bridge.

150. Sixteen choir boys of St Mary's church outside the south door of the church in 1865. One of them is the head boy who took the solo part of any particular anthem. There were usually 16 men in the choir combining alto, tenor, baritone and bass voices. Choir practices were held on mid-week evenings in the church. The choir boys practised in the morning before school hours in St Mary's Parish Hall in King Square. In my [P. J. Squibbs'] time as a choir boy the organist and choirmaster was Mr Frank Docksey.

51. (*right*) The Bridgwater, West of ngland and South Wales District Bank in ore Street, 1865, close to the present emises of Boots the Chemist at No. 34 ore Street. There were other bank pre-ises in the town including Messrs Sealy & ior's Bank on the Cornhill (which later ecame the Wilts and Dorset Bank and then loyds Bank), and Stuckey's Bank at York uildings.

52. (*below*) The south side of High Street 1865 showing the premises of Mr Joseph . Smith, Pawnbroker, and Mayor in 1868, 873 and 1874. Mr Smith is standing on the ght wearing a white apron. The gentleman uniform standing next to him is an army cruiting sergeant. This is now the site of *he Bridgwater Mercury* premises. A few ectators were interested in the photo-apher; photography was then, of course, uite an innovation.

153. The frozen River Parrett at Saltlands in 1895 during the bitterly cold February. The picture shows ships locked in frozen ice. The prolonged and severe frost brought about an almost entire cessation of outdoor labour in Bridgwater for some weeks, occasioning sore and widespread distress. A distress relief fund was started which enabled recipients to obtain supplies of bread, meat, groceries and coal, and soup kitchens and robin dinners were established.

154. The *Three Crowns Hotel* in St Mary Street in 1898, of which Mr Boyland was the proprietor. Next door there was another licensed house called the *Fleur de Lys*. At that time the town had so many licensed houses it was a wonder that they were a trading success, but one must assume that the proprietors were engaged in other activities to augment their living. The large posters on the wall refer to Sunday closing which was then much in the news. The last paragraph on one of the posters reads, 'Working Men; Defend your Rights'.

55. Looking down King Street, previously
alled Ball's Lane, in 1902. On the left is the
/esleyan chapel, a fairly large building, part
f which is in Dampiet Street. It was origin-
lly built in 1816 but was enlarged in 1860.
hop premises on the right behind the tree
ave been demolished and the site taken over
y the Roman Catholic church. There are
hildren standing about and on the left is a
ady on the pavement with an unusually-
haped perambulator. The Wesleyan chapel,
ow closed, has been sold to become a fur-
iture showroom.

56. The inside of St Mary's church in
865. The large oak screen across the
hoir stalls has now been removed and
rms the Corporation pews.

57. Decorations at the top of High
treet between the *Queen*, known
ocally as the *Round House* (no longer
n inn) and the *Valiant Soldier Inn*,
ooking towards Penel Orlieu in 1902
n the occasion of the Coronation of
ing Edward VII. The most elaborate
rchway must have taken hard work
nd considerable ingenuity to build.

158. (*left*) Looking towards York Buildings from the Cornhill in 1895. The corner of the *Royal Clarence Hotel* is on the left with Stuckey's Bank, now the National Westminster Bank, in the centre. Barton the Chemist's premises can be seen on the right (now part of the General Post Office, rebuilt in the 1970s). The road approaching King Square was then much narrower and though it was later widened it is still quite a bottleneck for traffic today.

159. (*below*) The river at Crowpill and the entrance to the Docks in 1902 with the large 'Glasshouse' or kiln on the Somerset Trading Company's premises in the distance.

160. A view of the river from Saltlands in 1880 with St John's church in the distance. The landing stages on the left were used principally for the loading of bricks, tiles and pottery goods for export, and for the importing of grain, timber and coal. No shipping comes up the river today and the landing stages have disappeared. It used to be very pleasant to walk along the river and seats were provided to rest awhile. There were brick and tile, pottery and the famous 'Bath Brick' manufacturers on both sides of the river in those days, but unfortunately they have all since closed.

161. A smashed waggon and the contents of bricks and tiles on the road outside the Cattle Market at Penel Orlieu in 1896 on the occasion of a serious strike by workers of the brick and tile industry.

162. A view of the River Parrett frozen over during the hard winter of 1895. To the right is Binford House now the site of the town's public library.

163. The river and its 'Bore' at Crowpill near the entrance to the Docks in 1902. The tidal wave is leading the salt water up the river, overcoming the downward flow of fresh water and turning the tide. The height of the 'Bore' varies, but is highest when high tides are accompanied by south-westerly gales.

164. A picture of the *Irene*, the last ship to be built and registered in Bridgwater. The vessel was launched from East Quay on 29 May 1907 by Mrs Bartlett of Seaton, Devon, a member of the Symons family of Bridgwater for whom the vessel had been built. The *Irene*, a ketch of 99 tons was built by the well-known firm of ship-builders F. J. Carver & Son at East Quay for the owners, Colthurst Symonds & Co. Ltd. of Bridgwater. She carried scores of the firm's bricks and tiles to many parts. In 1980 the reconditioned *Irene* was brought up the river as far as Combwich. In 1981 she was laid up in need of very serious repairs.

165. Part of St John Street looking from the entrance to Cranleigh Gardens in 1865, with a coachbuilder and wheelwright's business in the centre of the picture. There is a name board over the entrance to the coachbuilder's premises but it is indistinguishable. Some children and ladies in crinoline dresses stand in front of the houses.

166. A view from West Quay of the river with the two steam tugs, the *Petrel* and *Victor*, in 1865. During those days of prosperous shipping these tugs were used for hauling the vessels up and down the river.

167. The Rope Walk, Eastover in 1865, the proprietor of which was Mr J. H. Waddon, Mayor of Bridgwater in 1889. A disastrous fire occurred which led to the closure of these premises in 1951 and the subsequent disposal of the site to the Bridgwater Corporation. It is now a car park.

168. (*above*) Redgate House, Westonzoyland Road in 1865. An imposing residence which was usually occupied by people connected with farming. The site and adjoining grounds are occupied by the large factory of Messrs. Clark's Ltd., Boot and Shoe Manufacturers. About twenty-five years ago Mr Frank Bennett lived at Redgate House. He was a cattle dealer with a large business and the house, grounds and garden was looked upon as one of the most desirable in the town.

169. (*right*) The north side of High Street in 1892 showing the cobble-stone pavement in front of Beer's Cycle shop, Brown's Paint and Wallpaper shop and Smith, the Saddler. Two licensed houses, the *Bull and Butcher Inn* and the *Old Oak Inn*, are almost next door to one another. There are very few pedestrians or traffic about. This picture shows the full width of the High Street once the 'Island' of buildings had been removed.

170. The back and garden of a residence in King Street in 1865, now used as a doctors' consulting rooms, near the Wesleyan Methodist church. No doubt there were some attractive rare trees and shrubs in the well-kept garden and one receives the impression of the passing of prosperous, peaceful and leisurely days. The house was built by Richard Ball, the year unknown; in 1890 it was occupied by Joseph Thompson.

171. The West Somerset Yeomanry marching over the Town Bridge for embarkation to South Africa in 1899. In March, after an enthusiastic 'send-off' dinner at the Town Hall, as many as 21 of the Bridgwater volunteers, under Lt. W. S. Watson, left for active service. This constituted a much larger proportion of the population than any other town in the West of England. In 1900 the relief of the beleagured towns of Ladysmith and Mafeking was celebrated with great enthusiasm when the handsome sum of £208 5s. 7d. was raised for the Mafeking relief fund, the largest amount received from any town in the United Kingdom.

172. Manley the lamplighter in 1865, carrying his ladder and oil lamp. Most of the street lamps were on business premises and were lit with gas when it first came to the town on 22 May 1834. No doubt there were then very few street lamps and most of these would be in the main streets.

173. The south side of King Square looking towards Castle Street in 1865. The houses are much the same today bu in some cases the balconies have been removed and the cellars filled in. Most o the houses had back entrances in King's Place with stables. Railings surrounded the King Square garden but they have now been removed.

174. The Y.M.C.A. building, Eastover i 1898. This building was erected in 1887 to commemorate the foundation of the Young Men's Christian Association in Bridgwater in January 1859 by Sir George Williams. The building has now been demolished and shops have been erected there. It was originally the site o the old *Globe Hotel* which was destroye by fire in 1875.

175. T. Acland, Tobacconist, Statione Bookseller, Printer, Bookbinder and To Dealer in North Street, 1897, now a hai dressers' (No. 3 North Street). Advertis ments are much in evidence on the premises, especially for newspapers and tobacco, *The Western Morning News, The Bristol Times and Mirror, The Dail Press, The Morning News*; 'Redbreast' tobacco three pence per ounce, beware of imitation', 'Ogden's Plug' three penc per ounce packet; 'smoke '-------' cigarett five a penny'; 'Wills Gold Flake', 'Three Castles'; 'Westward Ho'; and Capstan Navy Cut tobacco. Acland sold Christm and mechanical toys as well and it must have been a thriving business. The businesses of Acland's retain the name and are now on the opposite side of the roa in North Street.

76. The Bridgwater Choral Society
ı the Town Hall in 1898. The picture
ıust have been taken during one of
ıeir rehearsals as there does not
ppear to be an audience in the bal-
ony. They gave numerous concerts
nd entertainments of this character
ere very popular and attracted large
udiences. There were, of course, no
inemas, wireless or television and
eople had to make their own amuse-
ıents and entertainment, due to
hich musical instruments of all kinds
ere in great demand. The writer's
ıother was one of the singers, and
ıe conductor then was a local chemist,
Ir Basker.

77. Decorations in St John Street in
883 on the occasion of the Bath and
Vest of England Agricultural Society's
how. On the right is the old *Queen's
Iead Inn* kept by Samuel Keirl, now
emolished to make way for Broad-
ay which leads to Blake bridge.
Iearly every street in the town was
ecorated in a similar manner on the
ccasion and the show was a great
ıccess throughout a week in May.

78. Looking down Fore Street from
ıe Cornhill in 1903. On the right is
ohn Whitby & Sons, Stationers and
ooksellers; next door was Hill, the
raper; then King & Son, Dining, Tea
nd Coffee rooms; then J. & M. Rich,
Vatchmakers and Jewellers; and then
ıe premises of the Wilts. and Dorset
ank. To the left were the offices of
obert Squibbs, Auctioneer and
state Agent, later the Home & Col-
nial Stores; next door was Shrimpton
Halson, Ironmongers; and then
ymons, Tailor and Outfitter. Today
he shop fronts have altered and new
usinesses are established, but the
idth of the street remains the same,
ıough with much more traffic and
ıany more people.

179. Bridgwater Great Western Railway Station in 1897, looking towards the 'up' line with the Goods department sheds in the distance. The *Railway Hotel* can be seen behind the Station. Passengers are on both sides of the station waiting for trains. There were many more passengers and trains in those days. Quite a number of station staff are evident and the station is looking generally tidy. There were then, of course, steam trains, which made frequent stops at the station; in addition the fares were very much lower and there were many more goods trains. Generally speaking the station looks much the same today.

180. St Matthew's Fair in 1906. Although the Fair had been held since before 1400, a local Act of 1857 made statutory provisions to accommodate the Fair. It was decided that it should be held annually on the last Wednesday in September for three days and that the venue should be the traditional one of St Matthew's Field. It was extended to Saturday in the late 1920s when bad weather so adversely affected business that the showmen were granted an extra day. Since then the final Saturday has become the most popular and well attended day of the Fair.

181. The river, Town Bridge and shipping in 1905 with quite a high tide.

182. Shops at Penel Orlieu in 1890, now the site of the Palace Theatre. A sweet and chocolate shop is on the left and on the right is Wills, picture framer and dealer. The Palace Theatre was opened on 8 March 1916 by Alderman Frank Wills, the proprietors were Alby Ward Theatres Ltd. The theatre was used for concerts, variety shows, plays and pantomimes and is now a cinema. It is one of two cinemas in the town today; at one time there were four or five including the Town Hall.

183. The premises of R. Squibbs & Son, the Bridgwater Furnishing Company at No. 27 Eastover in 1907, the proprietor of which was the author's father. They were extensive premises originally belonging to Messrs Roberts & Sons, the West of England Carriage Works, makers of horse-drawn vehicles and velocipedes (an early form of bicycle). The premises later became the Woolworth's of the town and are now St Catherine's Freezer Centre. In the days when Squibbs & Son were in occupation there were very large plate glass windows. The premises opposite, in New Road, were used by Mr Roe, the butcher, as a slaughterhouse and the sheep that were brought to the slaughterhouse had the habit of looking into Squibbs' shop windows and seeing their reflections in the mirrors of wardrobes and dressing tables. Astounded by this the sheep would often butt and smash the windows to the horror and amusement of all.

184. Wembdon Road looking towards the entrance to Northfield in 1900. There are no houses on the left and a lamp standard is almost covered by the high bushes. On the right can be seen the Wembdon Road Studio, an artist and photographer's business then owned by Mr O. C. Smith, later by Mr J. C. Hosier, then by Mr Montague Cooper and Mr S. W. Palfrey. The business closed on the death of Mr Palfrey. A large dog is lying in the roadway close to a bicycle at the kerbside. There is no traffic whatsoever.

185. Steele, the knife and scissors grinder in 1890, taken in Friarn Street. He was a familiar and well-known figure around the town in those days. The grinding stone was made to revolve by a foot pedal using a method similar to that of the old type of sewing machine.

186. (*left*) Taunton Road looking towards the town in 1865. Just one horse and cart on a rough road with cobble-stones at the edge of the pavement. In the distance to the right is the old Bridgwater workhouse. The residence to the left was occupied by Clifford Symons in 1890, a manufacturer of bricks, tiles and pottery goods.

187. (*below*) The police force of the town in 1890. It consisted of nine constables, two sergeants and the superintendent. In the back row of the picture are Constables Mead, Hubbard, Goodridge, Foster and Westcott; in the second row are Constable Potter, Sergeant Fish, Superintendent Lear, Sergeant Sheriton and Constable Lewis, and in the front are Constables Foster and Cull. Superintendent Lear, after more than half a century's service, was congratulated by the Bridgwater Corporation on his retirement with a superannuation allowance in 1893. The Borough Gaol and Police Station was then in High Street.

188. The original old *Hope Inn*, Taunton Road, in 1910 which was pulled down and rebuilt some years ago. It was a popular and well-patronised hostelry, almost opposite the old toll house and toll gates. The *Hope Inn* today is modern and very up-to-date. In years gone by, this old Inn was about the last house in Bridgwater on the Taunton Road.

189. A row of old houses in Monmouth Street in 1870 known as the 'Rookery'. They were situated at the entrance to Blake Place and on the west side of the Bristol road, in front of the grounds of St John's Vicarage. They were eventually demolished and a wall, railings and entrance gates were built surrounding the grounds of the Vicarage. Further along shops were built.

190. A picture of pupils of Dr Morgan's School with the Headmaster, the Rev. C. E. Lucette, in 1896. The Rev. Lucette resigned in 1899 and accepted the headmastership of Chard Grammar School. Mr William E. Catlow from St Albyn's School, Dulwich, then received the headmastership of Dr Morgan's School. He later became the Rev. W. E. Catlow, M.A. and was a most successful and highly-esteemed headmaster of the school. He retired after 24 years service and his valuable contribution to the public and to school and church life will long be remembered. Later a new Dr Morgan's School was built at Durleigh and the old school in Mount Street became the County Library Headquarters.

191. The house in Monmouth Street with the cross on the roof, in 1880, was the residence of the minister of the Bible Christian chapel which was in Polden Street but is now closed. Both the chapel and house are now occupied by Messrs Hamlins, the engineers. In 1882 the Minister was the Rev. W. Higman. He formed what was then called a White Ribbon Army and about eight hundred members enrolled. Crowded meetings were held in the chapel and elsewhere in the town and it was stipulated that all who joined the White Ribbon Army must be teetotallers. The chapel was built in 1876 with seating capacity for 250 persons. The house at one time was known as St John's Cottage.

192. Holy Trinity church, Taunton Road, in 1890. It is now demolished and a new church has been built at Hamp. This old church was built of stone in 1839, with a belfry containing one bell. Its interior was surrounded by a gallery. The Vicarage of Holy Trinity church was built in 1879 and has now been taken over by Sedgemoor District Council. There were seats in the church for 850 people and the register dates from 1839. In April 1892 the Sunday School and Parish Room of Holy Trinity church in St Saviour's Avenue was opened by the mayor and corporation; the building cost about £600.

193. Premises of D. Bradfield & Son, Monumental Stone Masons, in 1915 at the corner of Church Street (No. 57 Eastover). When this picture was taken 'to let' notices were in the windows. Mr David Bradfield was Mayor of Bridgwater in 1913, the year in which the Town Council first voted its Mayor a salary of £125 p.a. This occasioned many feelings of surprise and regret and some councillors thought that such a remuneration might lower the dignity of the office.

194. (*opposite above*) A sketch made by John Chubb in 1800 of the ruins of Bridgwater Castle. The building of this imposing structure began in 1200. A colossal mass of high walls and strong towers, it stood in the vicinity of King Street, Castle Street and close to the River Parrett. The whole site was surrounded by a deep, broad moat, 30 ft. wide, which brimmed with water at high tide. In 1645 under its Governor, Col. Wyndham, it withstood a three-day siege by Lord Fairfax of the Parliamentary forces, who destroyed its defences. The sole relic of the Castle today is the old Water Gate on the West Quay.

195. (*opposite below*) A sketch made by John Chubb *c.*1790 of the old stone bridge over the River Parrett. The bridge was built in 1395 and was very narrow; it was replaced by an iron bridge in 1795, which was, in turn, replaced by the present structure in 1883. The old bridge was triple-arched and hump-backed and small cottages crowded to the entrance on the east side. For a great number of years there were complaints that the three stone piers supporting the arches were a serious obstruction to the waterway.

196. (*above*) The first motor car to be seen in Bridgwater, owned by Mr Wesley Carter who lived at Portland Place, Wembdon Road in 1903. The car is a De Dion Bouton of six horse power, able to carry four persons, with an open roof, pneumatic tyres, a one hand steering device then known as 'tiller' steering, and presumably oil-lamp lighting. The man sitting in the car is Mr Wesley Carter and the man standing behind is Mr Harry Carver, the managing director of the Bridgwater Motor Company who supplied it. In addition to the two back seats, the other two passengers sat with their backs towards oncoming traffic in the two front seats.

197. (*above*) The small dock with the famous ol dredger, said to have been built by the renowned engineer Isambard Kingdom Brunel, passing through the bridge between the two docks in 1865. The old dredger was used until the docks were closed in 1970, to clear away the mud on the bed of the docks. The old dredger is a wonderful piece of engineering which was built in the 1840s and is still in working order. It is now preserved in the Maritime Museum at Exeter.

198. (*left*) The Congregational chapel, Fore Street in 1865. It has since been demolished and replaced by a supermarket. It was built in 1862 o grey limestone with dressings of bath stone. It could seat 900 people. In 1966 the new Westfield Congregational church, now the United Reformed church, was opened at a cost of £55,000 and has seating capacity for 366 persons. It was built to a modern design intended to fit in with other West Street buildings.

MAYORS OF BRIDGWATER, 1801-1967

1801	R. Codrington
1802	J. Symes
1803	J. Watson
1804	R. Anstice
1805	J. Allen
1806	R. I. R. Jenkins
1807	C. H. Burt
1808	W. Ford
1809	J. Mills
1810	T. Symes
1811	T. Pyke
1812	W. Inman
1813	J. Mills
1814	W. Ford
1815	W. Inman
1816	W. Inman
1817	R. Anstice
1818	J. Watson
1819	John W. Crosse
1820	J. R. Poole
1821	E. A. Stradling
1822	R. Woodland
1823	T. Symes
1824	J. Toogood
1825	R. Anstice
1827	E. Sealy
1826	R. Anstice
1828	J. Watson
1829	F. Axford
1830	W. J. Allen
1831	J. Evered
1832	Joseph R. Poole
1833	R. Anstice
1834	R. Woodland
1835	A. Southby
1836	T. W. Inman
1837	R. Ford
1838	R. Woodland
1839	T. Symes
1840	F. Axford
1841	R. Bagehot
1842	W. D. Bath
1843	W. D. Bath
1844	T. H. Watson
1845	J. Ruddock
1846	J. Sealy
1847	J. C. Parker
1848	J. Trevor
1849	J. Haviland
1850	R. Ford
1851	R. Ford
1852	T. Ford
1853	G. Parker
1854	W. Browne
1855	J. Browne
1856	W. D. Bath
1857	J. Ruddock
1858	J. Ruddock
1859	R. Woodland
1860	R. Ford
1861	J. Browne
1862	J. Browne
1863	J. Ruddock
1864	J. Browne
1865	J. Browne
1866	G. Parker
1867	J. B. Hammill
1868	J. R. Smith
1869	G. B. Sully
1870	G. B. Sully
1871	H. F. Nicholls
1872	H. F. Nicholls
1873	J. R. Smith
1874	J. R. Smith
1875	G. Wilton
1876	G. Wilton
1877	J. Leaker
1878	T. Collins
1879	W. T. Holland
1880	W. T. Holland
1881	C. Symons
1882	T. Collins (died)
	R. O. Backwell
1883	W. T. Holland
1884	F. J. Thompson
1885	A. Peace
1886	A. G. Barham
1887	A. Peace
1888	W. Hurman
1889	J. H. Waddon
1890	F. C. Foster
1891	H. Knight
1892	T. Manchip
1893	H. W. Pollard
1894	H. W. Pollard
1895	H. W. Pollard
1896	R. C. Else
1897	F. C. Foster
1898	T. Good
1899	T. Good
1900	W. Thompson
1901	W. Thompson
1902	W. T. Manchip
1903	W. T. Manchip
1904	H. W. Pollard
1905	H. W. Pollard
1906	H. W. Pollard
1907	H. W. Pollard
1908	F. Wills
1909	R. O. Sully
1910	H. W. Pollard
1911	H. W. Pollard
1912	P. O. Sully
1913	D. Bradfield
1914	D. Bradfield (died)
	F. G. Haggett
1915	F. G. Haggett
1916	F. G. Haggett
1917	F. G. Haggett
1918	F. H. Haggett
1919	S. Berry
1920	S. Berry
1921	S. Berry
1922	F. H. Allen
1923	W. H. J. Masding
1924	H. M. B. Ker
1925	W. Deacon
1926	W. Deacon
1927	W. Deacon
1928	F. O. Symons
1929	F. O. Symons
1930	F. O. Symons
1931	F. O. Symons
1932	C. Bryer
1933	C. Bryer
1934	F. J. Reed
1935	F. J. Reed
1936	F. J. Reed
1937	W. Chard
1938	J. Boltz
1939	L. H. Palmer
1940	R. Ashton
1941	R. Ashton
1942	R. Ashton
1943	H. Scholfield
1944	R. Chamberlain
1945	R. Chamberlain
1946	R. Chamberlain
1947	R. Washer
1948	R. Washer
1949	R. Washer
1950	E. Wills
1951	E. Wills
1952	P. Wills
1953	G. N. Hayball
1954	A. B. John
1955	R. Biddiscombe
1956	N. R. Gray
1957	W. O. Coate
1958	E. J. Davies
1959	Mrs A. B. Potterton
1960	J. G. Headford (died)
	Mrs A. B. Potterton
1961	A. D. Frost
1962	C. W. Milne
1963	G. C. Harris
1964	Mrs B. Davis
1965	Mrs B. Davis
1966	E. J. Davies
1967	L. Steer (died)
	G. C. Harris

MEMBERS OF PARLIAMENT FOR BRIDGWATER

1801 G. Pocock (sitting member)
J. Allen (sitting member)

1802 G. Pocock
J. Allen

1806 V. Poulett
J. Langston

1807 G. Pocock
W. Thornton

1812 G. Pocock
W. Astell

1818 G. Pocock
W. Astell

1820 W. Astell
C. K. Kemys-Tynte

1826 W. Astell
C. K. Kemys-Tynte

1830 W. Astell
C. K. Kemys-Tynte

1831 W. Astell
C. K. Kemys-Tynte

1833 C. K. Kemys-Tynte
W. Tayleur

1835 C. K. Kemys-Tynte
J. T. Leader

1837 H. Broadwood
P. Courtenay

1841 H. Broadwood
T. S. Foreman

1847 C. K. Kemys-Tynte
H. Broadwood

1852 C. K. Kemys-Tynte
B. S. Follett

1857 C. K. Kemys-Tynte
A. W. Kinglake

1859 C. K. Kemys-Tynte
A. W. Kinglake

1865 A. W. Kinglake
H. Westropp

1865 George Patton (vice H. Westropp, unseated) followed by:
P. Vanderbyl (vice G. Patton appointed Lord Advocate of Scotland)

1868 A. W. Kinglake
P. Vanderbyl

In 1869 Bridgwater ceased to be a parliamentary borough. All subsequent elections were held for the Bridgwater Division of the County of Somerset.

1885 E. J. Stanley

1886 E. J. Stanley (unopposed)

1892 E. J. Stanley

1895 E. J. Stanley (unopposed)

1900 E. J. Stanley (unopposed)

1906 H. G. Montgomery

1910 R. A. Sanders

1910 R. A. Sanders

1918 R. A. Sanders

1922 R. A. Sanders

1923 W. E. Morse

1924 B. Crompton-Wood

1929 R. P. Croom-Johnson

1931 R. P. Croom-Johnson

1935 R. P. Croom-Johnson

1938 V. Bartlett

1945 V. Bartlett

1950 G. Wills

1951 G. Wills

1955 G. Wills

1959 G. Wills

1964 Sir G. Wills

1966 Sir G. Wills

INDEX